WHAT CAN WE HOPE FOR?

ALSO BY JOHN POLKINGHORNE

Science and Christian Belief (1994)
The End of the World and the Ends of God (with Michael Welker) (2000)
The Work of Love: Creation as Kenosis (editor) (2001)
Quantum Theory: A Very Short Introduction (2002)
The God of Hope and the End of the World (2002)
Exploring Reality: The Intertwining of Science and Religion (2005)
Quantum Physics and Theology: An Unexpected Kinship (2007)
Science and Religion in Quest of Truth (2011)

What Can We Hope For?

Dialogues about the Future

John Polkinghorne and Patrick Miles
in conversation

Sam&Sam
Cambridge

First published in 2019
by Sam&Sam
29 Highfield Avenue
Cambridge CB4 2AJ
www.samandsam.co.uk

Typeset in Dante MT by James Miles

British Library Catologuing-in-Publication Data
A catalogue record for this book is available from the British Library

ISBN 978 1 9999676 1 1

Printed and bound by Amazon

2 4 6 8 10 9 7 5 3 1

eschatology *(theol)* *n* the doctrine of the last or final matters, such as death, judgement and the state after death [Gr *eschatos* last and *logos* a discourse]

(*The Chambers Dictionary*)

Now hope that is seen is not hope. For who hopes for what is seen? But if we hope for what we do not see, we wait for it with patience.

(Romans 8. 24-25)

CONTENTS

Foreword

John Polkinghorne needs no introduction: he is a highly respected scientist-theologian whose books on science and religion are read all over the world. I am a Russianist-writer with a lifelong interest in philosophy and religion. After my interview with John published in the *Church Times* of 9 October 2015 on the occasion of his eighty-fifth birthday, he proposed that I read *The Ends of the World and the Ends of God* (2000), edited by himself and Michael Welker, and his own shorter work *The God of Hope and the End of the World* (2002), which will be referred to in this book as *Ends* and *Hope* respectively.

I have to say that I have never speculated much about the end of the world and am not temperamentally suited to theology. However, I certainly agree with John Polkinghorne's statement in *The Faith of a Physicist* (1994) that 'we all need to form a world-view beyond the particularities of our individual disciplines'. *Ends* and *Hope* are extremely thought-provoking books. When John invited me to discuss their issues with him, I accepted with alacrity. Our conversation about them has lasted a year and been frank – as befits the seriousness of the subject. The journey John has taken me on has been unforeseen, intellectually exciting, even life-changing. My hope in editing our dialogues for the present book is that readers will be equally gripped by that journey.

I cannot thank John Polkinghorne warmly enough for his time, his patience, and the experience that this conversation has given me. The twelve sessions have, of course, been melded and moulded to form the five chapters of this book, but our words have hardly been changed at all. The whole book has been made possible by my son Jim's painstaking transcription of the original recordings, for which I thank him from the bottom of my heart. I am also extremely grateful to my wife Alison for checking the typescript and to Ruby Guyatt for verifying a quotation from Kierkegaard.

We thank Bloomsbury Publishing Plc and S.P.C.K. for permission to quote from *The Ends of the World and the Ends of God* and *The God of Hope and the End of the World*. The present book stands on its own, but it was stimulated by these two works and readers might well like to visit them.

Patrick Miles

Prologue

Science can tell us the story of the Universe, from its apparent origin in the Big Bang until the present day. It's a fascinating tale that it has to tell, which we should certainly take seriously. It speaks of how very delicately balanced interactions over a long period of time turned that initial ball of energy into the home of saints and scientists. This is a very important part of our understanding of the world. And it's also a story which seems to fit in quite well with a religious view of sense in the Universe, namely that a divine mind and purpose lies behind its unfolding fertility. It doesn't prove that, but it is at least highly consistent with it.

Well, that's one thing. But if instead of looking backwards we look forwards, science can also tell us about things in the future – not with the same degree of accuracy, but at least it indicates the general character of what is coming. And there the story is far from pleasing, in fact it's the story of eventual collapse and decay. The second law of thermodynamics says that *every system*, however orderly it may be at the beginning, will end up disorderly. The reason for that is that there are many, many more ways of being disorderly than orderly, so in the end everything decays.

When one tries to look at that fact from a religious point of view, it obviously produces some problems. What looked like a purposeful creation is seen to end up in collapse and decay. And that raises a very serious issue, which those of us who want to take seriously the insights of both science and religion have to take fully on board. Yet, on the whole, there has not been an enormous amount of discussion in theological circles about the significance of this. The Center of Theological Inquiry at Princeton ran a series of discussion meetings, called the Eschatology Project, in which the same group of people – some theologians, some scientists – met to talk about these problems. I was part of that project and enjoyed it very much. It produced a book which tries to tackle this issue, called *The End of the World and the Ends of God*. Later on I myself, benefiting from that experience, wrote a short book called *The God of Hope and the End of the World.*

The theological problem posed by the death of the Universe is very similar in quality to the problem posed by the existence of human death. If our lives are of great individual significance to God, then why do they end apparently in the decay of death? I think that is an issue that has to be treated with great seriousness.

My friend and neighbour Patrick Miles, having read these two books, visited me to discuss this, and we have had a number of interesting conversations about these issues. That has led us to have the temerity to think that others might like to at least listen in on the conversation, and so we have produced this book. We try to be honest and straightforward, not to sweep difficulties under the carpet. Although I don't for a moment pretend that all questions are answered, I think we can see that there is a sense in which it is quite possible to take science's view of the future seriously and not dispute the idea that the world is a divine creation. And we hope that this account of our discussions may be of help to other people who are pursuing these issues.

John Polkinghorne

1
The End of the Universe

Entropy – Steven Weinberg – Cosmology and eschatology – God's purposes are not magic – Making total sense of the universe – Christian loss of nerve – Science's contribution to eschatology – 'Metascience' – The scientific description of death – Continuity and discontinuity.

PM: John, these two books seem to propose a new eschatological dispensation, some might say cosmology, for our time. Why is this necessary?

JP: I think it's necessary because science has taught us a great deal about the past history of the universe, and can say in general terms quite a lot about its future. If things go on as they are at the moment, they could end very badly. That's the conclusion. And I think a lot of eschatological thinking has been very limited in terms solely of what has been happening on earth and on the timescale of a few hundred years. I think it needs to have a broader vision if it's really to make sense in our time.

PM: I suppose that's a very big difference between us, say, and even the nineteenth century. Would I be right in thinking that *geological* time was only discovered then?

JP: Absolutely. Associated with time, of course, is change, and associated with change also is decay in this sort of world. The second law of thermodynamics essentially says that in the end entropy always wins and the reason for that is simply that there are so many more ways of being disorderly than orderly. In the end, disorder always, always wins. The waters of chaos rise, and disorder wins the day.

PM: I am assuming that even brilliant scientific minds like Pascal 400 years ago, contemplating what he called the 'terrifying' silence and distances in space, still could not envisage that the universe would actually come to an end, although as a Christian he presumably believed in an 'eschaton', i.e. apocalypse and day of judgement?

JP: I'm not sufficiently sure about the history of it, but I think that's quite likely because people throughout history didn't realise that time is an index not just of when things happen, but also of *processes*, so that there is genuine change in the universe and that is something that I really think only struck people with the discoveries of evolutionary biology in the nineteenth century. I mean, God could clearly have snapped the divine fingers and brought the world into being ready-made and that of course is how people thought for a long time. But, first of all from biology, people learned that God, as Darwin's Christian friend Charles Kingsley said, has done something cleverer than bringing into being a ready-made world. God built a world so imbued with potentiality and fruitfulness that it could make itself creatures which could explore, bring to birth the potentiality with which God, the creator, had endowed creation.

PM: I absolutely accept that we are living in a qualitatively different age that calls for this rethinking. Do you feel, though, as my original question implied, that eschatological speculation has led to a more cosmological-astronomical view of ends and last things – that in fact your book *Ends* presents what used to be called a 'cosmology'?

JP: Well I think people have realised that God...that the action of the creator is not just to lay on the universe as a sort of backdrop to human drama but it's all part of one great unfolding process, and therefore questions of the ultimate fate of the universe in itself are of value and importance quite apart from the implications they might have for human life. My friend Steven Weinberg is a very famous cosmologist and also a very staunch atheist, and he has said that 'the more the universe seems comprehensible, the more it also seems pointless' – we know it's not going anywhere![1]

PM: Mmm...

JP: Except, if you like, into the rubbish bin, and I think that's a serious, serious challenge, and I think it's a challenge that many people feel in the present age. They feel that there is no *scientific* answer to that other than it's got to end in chaos. If there *is* a hope in the future, that hope lies not in the unfolding of present physical process but in the unrelentingly good purposes of the will of a creator. If we just stick with science, we are saying 'well let's make the best of it...we won't be here when it all collapses, so let's leave it at that'. But I'm not content to do that, and I think many people are not, either.

PM: But the interesting thing I find about that statement of Weinberg's is that he hasn't given up looking. Doesn't he go on to say in *The First Three Minutes* that the actual effort scientifically to understand the universe raises human life a bit above the level of farce and gives it 'some of the grace of tragedy'?[2]

JP: The instinct of a scientist – or indeed of any intellectually curious person – is to try to understand things as fully as possible and that means that you don't sort of smooth over the difficulties but you take them seriously.

PM: As a non-scientist, I found the contribution to *Ends* by William Stoeger, an astrophysicist from the Vatican Observatory Research Group, entitled 'Scientific Accounts of Ultimate Catastrophes in Our Life-Bearing Universe', very informative and sobering. Not only does he detail the ultimate fate of our sun and how, over trillions of years, 'the universe itself will eventually evanesce or possibly collapse in a final fiery conflagration (the big crunch)', he describes astronomical disasters that have occurred in the last hundred years or so, including when, over a number of days in 1994, twenty-one fragments of a comet crashed into Jupiter and exploded. He explains that if all of these fragments had impacted on Earth they would have wiped out life as we know it.[3] Well, this in itself raises a number of questions. First, do you in your heart of hearts think God would allow that?

JP: I don't know the answer to that. I don't think God would simply stop the asteroid or pieces of comet by poking a divine finger at them and saying, 'That's enough!' I believe God has purposes which will be fulfilled and that they won't be fulfilled in a magic way. I mean when you think about it, if God is the God of love, love always acts through respect for the beloved, and therefore allows in love a process of growth and development to be himself/herself, and that means that if the earth is to be obliterated by some asteroid it will not defeat God and his purposes.

PM: But if it wiped us all out, would that as it were philosophically change one's mind about the benevolence of God?

JP: It might. As I say, just as we don't believe that God acted in creation by snapping the divine fingers, so God acts if you like in redemption by not snapping the divine fingers either, but through the process of it. If an asteroid were to strike the Earth and produce terrible destruction and death, that would not be the end of everything. It would obviously be the end in terms of many presently existing material structures.

PM: The dinosaurs were *wiped out*.

JP: Exactly, exactly.

PM: But do you in your heart of hearts think God would do that?

JP: I don't know. All I would say is that if it happened that is not the last word.

PM: It would appear to be the last word for us!

JP: What you're asking on a grand scale is the simple question of what was

God's will in the Lisbon earthquake of 1755. Why on the day God didn't stop that? It was All Saints' Day, after all...

PM: This exercised the minds of Enlightenment thinkers like Voltaire, didn't it?

JP: Yes, in the eighteenth century it was very widely (and rightly) felt. I mean, this is wrestling with a problem. I say that if the problem has a solution then it is that the devastation of the earthquake is not the last word spoken.

PM: Coming back to Weinberg's famous statement that 'the more the universe seems comprehensible, the more it also seems pointless', one sees what he means, one understands why he says it, but he doesn't mention MAN: he talks of 'the universe', but what about people, what about *people* in the universe?

JP: I don't think we can be detached from our context in this sort of way.

PM: But he...his statement doesn't even mention human beings.

JP: Not the question as just stated, no. I mean human beings would be a sort of froth of meaning and sense of the universe, and again only transiently so. The froth is going to evaporate and that's it. The question is whether we can make TOTAL sense of the whole thing. And anything that has a relationship to the possible existence of God in relation to the universe is clearly not going to be a transient position.

PM: No. I recall that the conclusion of Stoeger's review of cosmological catastrophes is similar to the view you expressed at the begininning of this conversation: he says that whatever objects and beings the universe continues to bring forth they are 'temporary and destined to be replaced by others'.[4] But I found his contribution a bit fatalistic to be honest, because although these meteorite, asteroid and comet impacts are terrifying there aren't really that many of them!

JP: They don't occur all the time, obviously. That's presumably one of the conditions for a fruitful world. If it's always being annihilated or falling apart then it won't get very far; but equally that doesn't mean to say it will never be annihilated or fall apart.

PM: Yes. I do accept that the certain death of the universe is the departure point for a new, or expanded, eschatology. But there seems to me to be a misplaced focus on *cosmological* eschatology here. If we believe in life after death for ourselves (personal eschatology), why do we need to worry about the end of the universe?

JP: Well, I think that's back to this question of a purpose in the *whole* of creation. Does God have a purpose for the *whole* of creation, and does God care for the animals of the creation in a way that is appropriate to their natures? So as I said right at the beginning of our conversation, the universe is not just there to be the stage setting for the human drama, it is part of the whole story and God has purposes for his creatures. What those purposes are will depend on the nature of those creatures, obviously, but the whole thing is not just a sort of stage setting.

PM: But in theory at least – intellectually – the destruction of Earth by a 'stochastic' impact doesn't worry me, because I think 'well, if I am one of the people who is going to be destroyed tomorrow, now, in ten seconds, in thirty years, I still know that there is life beyond, that there is eternal life, because Christ said so'.

JP: We are all going to die in any case, yes. We might die in that way or we might die in our beds, but our personal destiny isn't the only aspect of eschatological need. The centre of the Christian faith is to accept both the reality of death and that it's not ultimate, because only God is ultimate and that is why the Christian hope is death and resurrection rather than just survival.

PM: So by analogy (which we know philosophers don't like) one cannot believe that there is nothing beyond the end of the Earth or the universe?

JP: I don't know whether one can or not, but the eschatological questions are really concerned with: 'Does the world make sense – complete sense?' Not just now, or for a while, but forever. The essence of Christian eschatology is the belief that through God and God's purposes and God's fulfilment of the divine purposes the world makes total sense. Not just now, but always, and that's the response to the Weinberg theme and so on.

PM: Can I approach this from another angle? You remember Gerhard Sauter's contribution to *Ends*, entitled 'Our Reasons for Hope'?

JP: Yes.

PM: He says there:

The mere idea that one day life on Earth will be brought to an end by some cosmic catastrophe is more terrifying than the traditional ideas of

the last judgement – even if one considers the fear of ending up on the wrong side of the final division. What is so terrifying about the new visions of destruction is that it all happens without someone who faces us, who confronts us. There is no other, there are only those left to destruction.[5]

This is presumably what would have terrified Pascal, who surely believed there was a second coming and a last judgement? Not to mention the fact that science invites us to believe that there is not just no *person* at the end of the universe, but *no thing*?

JP: Well it's as I said just now, only God is ultimate. In the end God and his Christ are not going to be defeated by death or by the inherent decay of the universe. It's an assertion of faith, in that sense.

PM: Sauter – a professor of systematic theology – has expressed very powerfully, hasn't he, quite viscerally and existentially, his *terror* at the scientific 'fact' that there will be no personalistic presence at the end of the universe, just annihilation? I am reminded of what Janet Soskice said in her contribution 'The Ends of Man and the Future of God':

I wish to suggest, especially but not only from the point of view of religious faith, that the crisis conflict of our modern period is not over knowledge – that our crisis, if it is such, is not epistemological so much as anthropological and as such a crisis of hope.[6]

Do you believe that there *is* this crisis, and do you agree with Janet that it's a question of hope?

JP: I think there's quite a deep human intuition of hope. But it's important to see that that's not just some simple pie-in-the-sky sort of hope. It comes after facing the facts, the scientific facts as we now know them, which is hard. So to that extent I agree with Janet, yes. And I also agree with the authors of *Ends* when they said that they believed it was 'of the highest importance that the Christians and the Christian church should not lose nerve in witnessing to our generation about the eschatological hope that is before us'.[7]

PM: Do you believe there *has* been such a loss of nerve among Christians (as opposed to non-believers)? If so, why?

JP: Yes. I think that a lot of people – including some people in the church – have lost their nerve about this, and I think there are basically two reasons for it. One is that, actually, the only ground for a destiny beyond death is the faithfulness of God and I think that we've got a sort of weakened understanding of that. But the other thing – and one of the things I've tended to write about – is that we ask ourselves 'does it make SENSE to talk about a destiny beyond death?'. You know, here I am, I'm a complicated collection of molecules, I die, they will all be dispersed, in what sense do I survive? I am blown in the wind. And I think that's the question of continuity and discontinuity. If there's no continuity of any kind then it's just a question of whistling in the dark.

PM: Well, this is why I think your application of modern scientific understanding of *process* is very important.

JP: I think so.

PM: We will be discussing it, of course, but could I first ask you something about the terms of reference of *Ends*? You see, one of the things that fascinated me about both books, *Ends* and *Hope*, was the concepts of metaphysics and meta*science*. What can science contribute to eschatology, which is by definition metaphysical speculation?

JP: Well, I think science doesn't determine metaphysics, but it certainly constrains it. Whatever our future destiny is, it cannot be just a repetition of the present destiny. So there will be change, but there must also be continuity, otherwise what happened first becomes irrelevant to what happened subsequently. Science has something to tell us about how the present world works. I mean we have learned that in this present world, the world of evolving complexity, theologically interpreted God works through process rather than just through divine snapping of the fingers and perhaps science gives some sort of hold on that idea.

PM: And you feel that, in particular, developments in quantum physics – entanglement, relationality, complexity theory for instance – intriguingly suggest at least avenues of continuity or possibilities?

JP: Yes. What the discovery of quantum theory has made clear is that whatever the world is, it's not a world of mechanism, and of course in a world of mechanism our future destiny means winding up the clock again or something like that, so there must be *development* in that sense. By 'metascience' I mean just some sort of picture. We talk all the time about development, the pattern-forming concept of information, and so on, and that's, if you like, a 'metascience'.

PM: Well, I think 'metascience' is almost a neologism, as I couldn't find it in any dictionary.

JP: No, probably not. But one needs a word for that kind of picture, metaphysical or theological, that science gives us a lead to or a hold on.

PM: Thank you, John. That has really clarified it. In a way I was surprised that the contributors didn't make more claim for science and its relevance to eschatological continuity than they did. They were more tentative than I was expecting, more theological than I was expecting.

JP: Yes, but science doesn't tell you everything and in a sense the whole CTI Eschatology Project starts from a recognition that if science does tell you everything then in the end it all ends badly.

PM: A different way of putting this question is that it didn't actually strike me what the scientific input to the volume or the three-year project was. *Ends* is subtitled, of course, 'Science and Theology on Eschatology', but as far as I could see, of the seventeen contributors only you, William Stoeger, and the neurophysiologist Detlef Linke, are scientists, the rest are theologians. One might conclude that the scientific component to the dialogue and discussion was slight.

JP: But you would be quite wrong to think that. The input of the scientists is that they 'pose' the whole question 'What are the prospects for the future?', and if we rely on science only to answer that then the answer will be bad. People have this instinctive feeling that there must be meaning to the thing, that it can't all just be a tale told by an idiot, full of sound and fury. And what I'm saying is that science sharpens up the realisation: if that's the case – I mean people's instinctive feeling – then there must be more to be said about it than science can say. In other words science opens a space that has to be filled if we're going to make complete and satisfying sense of the whole thing; a space which will not be filled simply by scientific insight. We live in a very rich world and I believe in the presence of an infinitely rich creator. So all the particular disciplines, whether they are logic or empirical science or whatever they may be, are insights into the truth and not the whole thing. It's a bit like the insights we have into people's characters. Science constantly informed, if you like, the regular meetings of the project. The existence, the reality, of modern science was always a context of our discussion.

PM: Ah, thank you, I understand now. I was also interested that William Stoeger made a specific scientific intervention in addition to his astrophysical one. He said that 'denying the scientific description of death is not an option'.[8] What *is* the scientific description of death?

JP: The scientific description of death is the failure of the body to function and its subsequent disintegration and so on. That's the description, and it looks like *the end*. What was there is no longer there, and that's why the question of continuity and discontinuity comes in.

PM: Yes, but even as a non-scientist I can see that that's not a scientific description of *death*, it's a medical description of *dying*, or a chemical description of decomposition. It seems to me that even in pragmatic, rational terms there is more to death than that. To some it may 'look' like the end, to others it may 'look' like something else. I remember when a friend of mine's first child was born, he was there, which was quite unusual at the time, and he said to me afterwards: 'Patrick, I don't understand it, it was totally mysterious... Where did this *come from*? I know how this baby was made, but where has it come from? It's not exactly a miracle, but I don't understand the continuity of this child, its continuity back through time.' So he felt the child had come from somewhere. And I've had the experience when I've been with people who have died. I've had the plain experience that their body is dying but, just as the baby came from somewhere, I've had a gut feeling that they're *going* somewhere.

JP: I'm not sure the baby analogy is very helpful. We know where babies come from –

PM: Ha!

JP: – we know about fertilisation and that sort of thing, we know that their DNA is formed by amalgamation and so on and so on. We know, if you like, the basic information-content of that baby.

PM: But their continuity through time...goes to the beginning of time.

JP: Beginning of time?

PM: Genetically, it must go back –

JP: Well no, we're genetically different from our children and from our ancestors.

PM: But there is a continuity of flesh, isn't there, as it were?

JP: Well there is a degree of continuity, yes, yes, that's right.

PM: So I don't see why we assume this mysterious continuity is going to end. To end in 'death'.

JP: It's both continuity and discontinuity.

PM: That's certainly how it seems to me.

JP: I am genetically distinct from my mother and father, though I am clearly *connected* with my mother and father.

PM: Yes. I suppose I don't mean so much 'genetically' as evolutionarily, developmentally, in terms of process. We have, we are the bearers of, a continuity that stretches back millions of years to very primitive organisms. In fact we are made of star dust? So why should we jump to the conclusion that this process as old as the universe is going to end in death and our 'returning' wholly to dust, rather than changing into something else? My *apprehension* is much more of the continuity than of the discontinuity, even though I have witnessed several deaths. It's a very strange thing... And you want to involve process in the discontinuity / continuity of death, don't you?

JP: Yes. Death is the irreversible cessation of the processes that keep the body working, and it's very important to see that resurrection is not resuscitation, it's not just reassembling the bits and pieces and letting them tick away for a bit longer.

PM: Well, I know the subject of death is absolutely central, and I know we will be addressing it very soon, but I have some more questions about eschatology before we get there.

JP: That doesn't surprise me. Fire away!

2

Is Eschatology Necessary?

Attitudes to eschatology – 'Thought-experiments' – Michael Polanyi – 'Motivated belief' – Mathematicians and Plato – The cloud of witnesses – The Book of Revelation as symbols – The Harrowing of Hell – Eschatology and utopias – The 'ethical demands of the present' – Kathryn Tanner – Eschatology as the keystone of the Christian building? – Death as the biggest threat to religious belief.

PM: I think this may amuse you. Someone was asking me what our conversations were about. I said, 'Eschatology.' '*Escapology*?' they queried.

JP: Ha!

PM: Of course, they had just misheard me. But there *is* a certain feeling amongst people that eschatology is a form of escapism from the present, isn't there? I mean, many people will say that the *present* is hopeless enough.

There is war in the Middle East of almost unheard-of brutality, Russia is stirring up 'hybrid' war on Europe's borders, the EU is foundering, America and China seem on course for conflict, in Africa there is one humanitarian disaster after another, states have various forms of weapons of mass destruction, ecological catastrophe seems just round the corner. What would you say to people who felt that speculation about the life beyond and the end of the universe is academic and superfluous – people who yearn for hope about the present?

JP: There is a disorientation, a fragmentation...a deeply conflicted state in human affairs, I'm not going to deny that. If you feel there is no unfolding fulfilment then you feel driven just to grab what you can along the way. Hope about the present is a part... Eschatology isn't a sort of pie in the sky joy for everybody instantly like that. It says there are struggles, there are disappointments, there are puzzles and so on but there is no reason to think that it is not part of an unfolding and shaping process and therefore, you know, you can't have it all at once. You could grow into it.

PM: Well actually I was very interested to see the range of attitudes to eschatology that feature in *Ends* and *Hope*. For instance, in his contribution to *Ends*, 'Contingent Futures: Imagining the Ethics of Cosmology', Larry Bouchard writes that 'the physical cosmos is relevant mainly as the contingent arena for our pilgrimage with God. That it will end comes as no theological surprise'.[1] I thought exactly that when I read your and Michael Welker's statement in *Ends* that 'this scientific insight of the twentieth century poses a great threat to theology and the faith of all religions'.[2] How can this be, I thought, if these religions have always had their world-endings and their life-affirming theodicies? What has changed?

JP: I think the change is that the certainty about the world we live in at the moment is that it is of long but limited duration and it isn't going to end in simple direct terms 'well' but 'badly'. It's going to either fall apart or die of exhaustion. The point is that we now know the world and the universe have a history, but the timescales of that history are very long and almost incomprehensible to the finite human mind. And that means that the ordinary sort of thinking of one thing after another isn't going to solve the problem.

PM: Yes. As we discussed last time, the subject has been changed by the scientific discovery of the life of the universe and of earthly time...geological time...cosmic time. But in the old days it used to be thought that the end of time would be marked by the appearance of the Antichrist. What has happened to the Antichrist?

JP: The picture of a sudden appearance of real opposition – a final resurgence of evil – and then the defeat of the opposition, is not a way in which we think about these things at the moment. Part of the point about the two books, *Ends* and *Hope*, is to articulate what that could mean.

PM: But of course there was a time when Christians spoke of *science* as the Antichrist...

JP: Well I mean yes. Christians have always tended to be a bit liberal in attaching that label to people they don't like!

PM: Yet today one can even adduce science in eschatological speculation... For instance, in *Hope* you conclude from modern chaos/complexity theory that the carrier of continuity in our bodies is the 'immensely complex information-bearing pattern in which that matter is organised'. You actually say that 'this information-bearing pattern is the soul'.[3] People might think that your attempt to involve science in substantiating 'continuity' in Christian eschatology is a bit like the Edwardian physicist Oliver Lodge's attempt to use 'psychical research' as scientific proof that humans survived beyond death. Could not both attempts be described as simply the responses of scientists to a crisis in *belief*, in faith?

JP: The trouble – I agree – is the persistent temptation, or indeed the need, to put God to the test. You know, 'come on, if you're there, show yourself', 'turn this water into wine', or whatever it might be. And that is an attempt at 'magic'.

PM: Of course, what I think Lodge was really looking for, *searching* for, was religion. He was looking for religious belief in an age of 'scientific' materialism.

JP: Anyone who's searching for some deeper understanding that makes the world make more profound sense is looking for a religion in some sense.

PM: Yes. In some sense.

JP: But this talk of the soul as an information-bearing pattern is, of course, hand-waving, because the pattern isn't just the properties of molecules and that sort of thing, it's something that's more dynamic than that. There are characters involved – ourselves, God, and so on – so it's just a question of how you think about these things, and the modern study of chaotic systems – of systems near to the edge of chaos I should say – where they generate patterns and maintain patterns in that sort of way, is at least, I think, a helpful launching in this direction. And we're just struggling to find language that begins to be adequate to talk about it. Our conversation has come back to what I call 'metascience'. If I suggest, as I do in *Hope*, that the nature of the post-resurrection appearances of Christ could derive from the intersection of the spacetime of the old creation and the spacetime of the new, which mathematicians would have no difficulty in thinking of as being in different dimensions of the totality of divinely sustained reality, then that's just some sort of picture, it's metascience. It's a thought-experiment.

PM: How do you see or define a 'thought-experiment'?

JP: A thought-experiment is a way of trying to see a consistency or fruitfulness of a thing without going into all the details that be required for a realistic account of it. It's a halfway stage between having an idea and having the idea worked out to see if it all hangs together and what its consequences might be. And it's very useful in science and I'm sure in other things as well.

PM: I associate thought-experiments more with science than with theology, but do you think they are quite legitimate in both – in eschatology, for instance?

JP: Yes, I think it's a technique that's not just useful in scientific terms but for exploring in any sort of thought. I mean supposing you were thinking about some organisation of political or economic life and you have to ask yourself, would it be likely to work? And rather than embarking on a full-scale indulgence in it, it's a good idea to do some thought-experiments on it. For instance, if you have a system which guarantees that nobody *needs* to work then will anybody work?

PM: That's a very good example! Well I think what gave me cause to think about this subject is that obviously in science, or even in politics, you start with a certain empirical set...you start with a certain empirical situation...but in theology, or religion, I'm not sure what that basis is.

JP: Well, certainly one's trying to think about the unthinkable if you like; the infinite reality of God. And all pictures of God, all attempts to understand God's relationship for example to suffering in the world, are thought-experiments, in the sense that we haven't got it all tied up.

PM: Something that I feel is connected with this theme is your concept of 'motivated belief'. What *is* 'motivated belief'?

JP: Motivated belief is belief in which we have to understand that the *reason* for thinking it – a reported fact, one's own experience, whatever it might be – is right. You see, first I want to say a bit about Michael Polanyi. Polanyi was a very distinguished physical chemist, but he turned to philosophy in his later life and he wrote a – I think still very influential – book called *Personal Knowledge*.[4] In the preface, he says that he is writing the book to see how he can commit himself to what he believes to be true whilst knowing that it might be false. And there is a certain tentativity about all human exploration. This was sensationally exemplified by the mathematical philosopher Gödel's discovery. Gödel showed that no axiomatic system which is complicated enough to contain real numbers can demonstrate its own consistency. Nevertheless, most of us I think don't find it difficult to commit ourselves to the belief that the real numbers are a consistent thing. So there is an element of involvement in that, an element of commitment, and it's not a *rash* commitment in the sense that, you know, you believe you are going to win the lottery next week...that type of belief.

PM: So it's not totally subjective.

JP: Exactly. There is reason for it, if you like. But the reason, as I say, is not a proof. I can't say to you that you're stupid if you don't believe this or that, because you're merely missing something which is very important, and Polanyi is saying...he's talking about science in this book and – like all scientists – he believes that science is bringing us real knowledge and he commits himself to that knowledge. Commitment is a very important word for Polanyi, you aren't just an uninterested spectator, you commit yourself to believing it to be true. I think that's a very helpful insight. The number of things that we know absolutely is limited. Thinking about Gödel again, we might have said that one thing for certain is that mathematics, the real numbers, for heaven's sake they're real! But it wasn't quite as easy as that.

PM: But can there be such a thing as 'motivated truth'?

JP: I think motivated truth would be a sort of – almost an oxymoron.

PM: It would seem to come very dangerously close to saying 'it's true because I want it to be true'.

JP: Yes, well absolutely. If I've used that phrasing then I repent.

PM: No, no, you haven't used it at all. I just found myself thinking in that direction because I don't think most people, perhaps, when they read our interview in *Church Times*, understood what motivated belief is. You said there that you felt 'ultimately, all physical theories – and, in fact, I think, all human understandings of the nature of reality – have an element of commitment to a point of view that is not logically coercive'.[5]

JP: I owe that thought to Polanyi really.

PM: What about the words 'not logically' coercive? That may have shocked a few people!

JP: Well the Gödel example shows how subtle the nature of logical consistency is. And we shouldn't forget that. That's why I'm never very sympathetic to the people who found G.K. Chesterton so helpful. I don't think one should revel in paradox.

PM: It seems to me – and you may have to correct me here – that for mathematicians a paradox, for instance 'Russell's Paradox', is simply something that they decide they need to look at more carefully and demonstrate is not a paradox but a contradiction based on a false assumption.

JP: Yes, yes. The same of course in the physical world is true of wave / particle duality. And that's the *motivation* for investigation.

PM: So why do you think it is so important today to recognise the concept of motivated belief?

JP: It's because the motivation also drives you – motivation from experience and so on – drives you in directions you wouldn't have anticipated. I mean, it would be very easy to construct a proof that something couldn't sometimes look like a wave and sometimes a particle. Particles are condensed, point-like things, a wave is spread out and oscillating. Nevertheless, quantum theory says that that's what light is like, and after about twenty-five years of struggle, the physicists, through Heisenberg and Schrödinger, were able to see how that could be so. And it could be so because the world is not as unproblematically objective as people actually thought at the time. I think that would very much surprise Plato, but would please him probably when he thought about it a bit.

PM: Thank you, John, thank you very much indeed. I think I am getting there. I think what could throw a lot of people is your phrase 'not logically coercive', because I think they perhaps believe that the idea something in the sciences is not logically coercive is just an initial appearance, that if you look more closely it's always logical.

JP: Well it has to have its own logic.

PM: Yes, perhaps that's what I mean.

JP: What we mean by 'relatives' in this case is that there isn't a universal logic, which applies to everything. And the logic of a lot of quantum mechanics, for example, is something that *nobody* would have thought of, about the nudge of nature in that direction.

PM: Yes, absolutely. Absolutely. Why, by the way, do you say in *Ends* that mathematicians are 'instinctive Platonists'?[6]

JP: I think they are instinctive Platonists in the sense that they believe there is a world of mathematical truth they are exploring. And they commit themselves to that belief and to the results of that exploration. They don't think that mathematics is just an arbitrary human confection. It is really there in some sense. The Polanyi stuff shows that that inspiration is not quite as straightforward as just walking through the forest and counting the trees...

PM: And of course, I suppose if you believe there is a world of mathematical truth, then it's only a small jump to believing, as Plato or Socrates did, that these 'forms' are somewhere. That they are located somewhere.

JP: Yes, and of course the Christian answer to that would be 'in the mind of God'.

PM: In fact I was intrigued to see you say in *Hope* that it would be possible to reconcile the information-bearing-pattern concept of the soul with 'a highly modified form of Platonism' because the 'information-bearing patterns of the soul could be considered as intersecting with the everlasting realm of mathematical entities', where they would 'remain lodged after the decay of the body'.[7] But it is a very rarefied and static world, isn't it, the world of mathematics and Platonism, or the Platonic world of mathematics?

JP: Yes and no, in the sense that the richness of mathematics – the variety of mathematical systems – is, I suppose, the discovery of the last century or so and it's not just like going through the forest encountering the trees.

PM: No. But do you think mathematicians *realise* that they are instinctive Platonists?

JP: No, no. I don't think that's a relevant question! Some do, some don't, I suppose is the answer to that.

PM: But you are certainly not a Platonist yourself, are you?

JP: I'm not a Platonist in a pure sense, no. I prefer a thorough-going psychosomatic picture of human nature. But I don't think the old man was completely mistaken.

PM: Mm. I remember that Kierkegaard said Plato's ideas about the immortality of the soul really are profound, and 'reached after deep study', but that he has no authority for them![8] Turning back now, John, to the wide fan of views about eschatology represented in *Ends* and *Hope*, I must say I was staggered by the reduction performed by your scientist-theologian colleague Arthur Peacocke. As far as I can see, he makes no appeals whatever to science or metascience. He asks 'What is the cash value of talk about "a new heaven and a new earth"?' and answers it himself:

The only propounded basis for this seems to me to be the imaginings of one late-first-century writer (in Revelation) and the belief that the material of Jesus' physical body was transformed to leave the empty tomb. The latter is at least debatable and the former can scarcely be evidence. So what is left is belief in the character of God as love and that God has taken at least one human being who was fully open to the divine presence into the divine life – the resurrection and ascension of Jesus. Is not all the rest of Christian eschatology but empty speculation?[9]

These are hard words, aren't they, from a scientist and a theologian?

JP: Well, I respect his scrupulosity, and I agree that belief in God as love and in God's faithfulness is the only ground for a destiny beyond death. But I also believe that we can look at how that faithfulness has been acted out in history and might be beyond history. We can practise thought-experiments about this; we can seek 'motivated belief' about the 'cash value' of the old and new creations. As I said in *Hope*, in both science and theology our anticipations of the future are influenced by our understandings of the past and present.

PM: Apropos of that, in the introduction to *Hope* you explain that it is fundamental to your discussion to appeal to 'the revelatory insights by which the divine character has been made known' and then you use this phrase 'the record of the particularly transparent people and events through which God has graciously shown forth the divine nature'.[10] Could you elaborate on the word 'transparent', on the idea of 'transparent'?

JP: Most of us live in a rather hazy notion of the divine presence. I mean our experiences are not profound, they are encouraging but not usually deep. People who are *transparent*, I suppose, are people who really know the presence of God in their lives and really trust the goodness of God. And you meet such people – two or three I've known – who without being ostentatiously pious are people who clearly are living in the belief that God loves them, and I often think the more deeply and firmly we ourselves can believe that, correspondingly transforms our lives in being.

PM: Well I think I know what you mean because I had that experience with many believers in Russia, under Communism –

JP: Of course, yes.

PM: – when the full power of the state was being brought to bear to destroy belief and yet there were fairly simple people who had a complete belief and you found it was shining through them. But you would presumably include in this cloud of witnesses the saints of the past, the prophets...

JP: Of course, yes. I mean scripture is, if you like, the record that comes to us of the encounters of people who have known God more clearly than most of us do. And of course we believe that is particularly true of Jesus, because Jesus is himself divine and a man. I mean, if you ask the question, 'does God love me?', then ultimately the Christian answer is to say, 'did Jesus love the people in need who crossed his path?', and the answer is, I think, yes he did.

PM: But when you come down to it, isn't Christian *eschatology* hopelessly confused? Or at least, don't you think most people are hopelessly confused by it? On the evidence of the New Testament, they may believe that they go to another life 'in the twinkling of an eye', but then there is also Judgement, and Heaven and Hell, whilst, on the basis of one man's writings in a cave on Patmos nearly two thousand years ago, *back on Earth* there is still the Antichrist to come, Armageddon, the Apocalypse, the 1000-year Rule of Saints, the creation of God's Kingdom on Earth, the Second Coming, the general Resurrection, and the New Jerusalem. How do all these scriptural eschatons fit together? Does anyone know? Isn't it a bit of an eschatological MESS?

JP: So, your first question is about various New Testament statements. The first thing I want to say is that it's possible that everybody goes through the life of the world to come at the same point *there* and leaves – of course – this world at different times. That may be what 'the twinkling of an eye' means. The other thing I want to say is that all these things you mention here – the Antichrist, Armageddon etc – these are powerful symbols but they're not a sort of blow-by-blow account of the future. So I think there are puzzles here, but I don't think there's real difficulty.

PM: I see. But do you think people are confused?

JP: Well of course people are confused, but they need to think straight about it! And decide what are the important things. The important thing is whether life continues, whether it continues in a fulfilling way and in the clearer presence of God. These symbols all relate to that, but as I say I don't think they are detailed descriptions of exactly what's going to happen.

PM: So perhaps they relate outwards to us, but not to each other? They are *symbols* that were never intended to join up, perhaps?

JP: Yes, these are rather a miscellaneous collection of symbols. You've got to remember that people in the New Testament were groping to understand these things and so it isn't a well worked out sale's pitch, to use Peacocke's imagery.

PM: But so many wonderful things are recorded as *happening* in the New Testament, for example God speaks from the sky, people are raised from the dead, Christ walks on water, that it is understandable, isn't it, that for centuries people have taken the eschatological statements of the Book of Revelation literally?

JP: Well, thinking for myself, that's just too literal and unimaginative. For instance, outside certain, often American, sects, the rule of the saints and so on is not much of a *contemporary* issue. There's this delicate matter of not taking things literally in a flat-footed way but equally not saying we can't say anything. These apocalyptic images were thought-experiments of the time, they were exploratory images. I mean, the coming of Christ is not, I think, the heavens being split open and a figure attended by angels coming down, it's the way of thinking about how, *ultimately*, will the lordship of Christ be brought about in this world? As St Paul says, at the moment we do not see everything subject to him, 'under his feet'.[11] Nevertheless there is hope for it. You're just trying to think, is that hope negated by the presence of evil? So I think it's particularly important to read the Book of Revelation in this sort of way. Otherwise...I mean Revelation is full of images that are only partially satisfactory – a sort of vengeance-full God and so on – but I don't think the author was completely satisfactory, and he clearly wasn't the author of John's gospel, it's a different, another writer.

PM: Surely. A powerful and canonical subject of Russian icons is Christ's 'Harrowing of Hell'. How do you see this eschatological image?

JP: The harrowing of hell is an exploratory image which doesn't go directly to the words of Jesus that we know about, and which I don't find very helping and so on. I have a feeling that it really burgeoned in the Middle Ages, but I'd have to look that up somewhere. On the other hand, it's always been the *core* of Christian thinking that when we say Jesus was made man we mean it in a really rather literal sense, a sense of 'he shared human experience to the full'. As St Gregory of Nazianzus said in the fourth century, 'what has not been shared has not been redeemed'. Jesus really enters into human life, he doesn't pay a sort of interesting visit to see what it all looks like, he *shares* that. It's very important that when we say Jesus died we really mean he died. And he was buried. So he *shared* in human death as part of the process by which he triumphs over human death. Holy Saturday – the gap between Good Friday and Easter – is badly neglected in a lot of contemporary Christian practice and thinking. It's not a convenient day off to get the church decorations right, it's an essential part of the experience.

PM: This phrase 'he descended into hell' really just means he was dead, then?

JP: First of all it's Hades, not hell – it's the place of the dead, Sheol, not a place of torment. So yes, it simply means he was really dead, dead exactly the way we shall be. That's terribly important.

PM: I think the translation has confused a lot of people... And I can see why you describe the whole elaboration of this into the harrowing of hell, the releasing of Adam and Eve and the patriarchs etc, as simply an 'exploratory image'.

JP: Of course, modern liturgies and modern bibles don't use it. For them 'hell' in this context is either 'Hades' or 'a place of the dead', or something like that.

PM: Right. Well if Arthur Peacocke seems to make minimal claims for Christian eschatology, Karl Barth seems to go to the other extreme... In *Hope* you quote him as saying: 'Christianity that is not entirely and altogether eschatology has entirely and altogether nothing to do with Christ.'[12] Doesn't this suggest that Christianity is some sort of 'other-worldly' Utopia?

JP: No. It's important to see that we're not talking about simply a 'wiping the slate clean', a creation of a new Utopic world in which everything is wonderful and all of the problems of the old world aren't there. If that were the case, then of course the immediate question is why bother with the present world? So eschatology in the wider sense is not concerned with pie in the sky, but is concerned with God's unfolding processes that go into this world and continue to complete it in life beyond death. I think what Barth is saying is simply that if you just take the present life, it's not very convincing that God has a purpose for creation.

PM: I see.

JP: It's a sort of 'toy-game' that God plays for a bit and it's sort of fun, but then you pack it up and put it away.

PM: I understand. Yet 'eschatology' for most people is just an abstract term, and words like 'futurology' and 'utopia' have become so political.

JP: Those imply ameliorations, if you like, within the present process. And they dodge the question which loomed high in our CTI deliberations about the end of the world and the ends of God, which is what do you make of the fact that the present world is completely bound to end in chaos and decay, that in Weinberg's word the universe seems 'pointless'?

PM: I notice that towards the end of *Hope* you yourself say that 'eschatology is the keystone of the edifice of theological thinking, holding the whole building together'.[13]

JP: I had forgotten I said that. It's a little bit of an over-statement, I think. But I think eschatology is very important. If it's missing, you know, the Christian building collapses. But I wouldn't want to give the impression that it's the only thing, or the principal thing.

PM: Well I fear the operative word is 'theological', isn't it? The keystone of *theological* thinking...

JP: Yes!

PM: And of course many people *don't* accept theology, that is the trouble.

JP: What we're discussing is when we look at the nature of the reality in which we are a part, do we see any reason to believe there *might* be a divine mind and a divine purpose in this? You're working on the question of CREDIBILITY of a theological attitude to the world. And, as I say, if the world is just a transient blip that seems to me to be in some sense – in the longest, most profound sense – 'pointless' as my friend says, then this theological attitude is very important. If it's not important to you, then I can't force you to believe that it is.

PM: In *Hope* you refer to 'a kind of other-worldly piety that neglects the ethical demands of the present'.[14] But surely, the *ethical* demands of the present are precisely what a lot of people believe religion to be about? They believe that Christ's message is about the now, in other words 'the ethical demands of the present'? They are suspicious of theology as something 'other', a system of abstract concepts perhaps, something we are even told students can study without believing in, a building in which people do not need spiritually to *live*? I would have thought most Christians' view is very grounded in ethics and present moral choice about their own and wider human life. Personally, I think this is why the state of the world, this world now, depresses some of them much more than the cosmological prospect of some future end of the world. They have always known that the world was going to come to an end, because Christ said so.

JP: Well we're back to what has been the reiterative theme of our discussion this morning and that is TOTAL SENSE; and the 'pie in the sky' interpretation, it seems to me, doesn't have that. It just says, 'it's terrible now and there's the reward coming at the end'. That seems to me *very* unsatisfactory.

PM: Yes. Well my quotation from *Hope* about the ethical demands of the present comes from the section where you have been discussing Kathryn Tanner's ideas.[15] You know, of 'realised eschatology', present transcendent eschatology, really. So your answer doesn't surprise *me*...

JP: Well, I can only give that answer, I can't ADJUST it –

PM: No...

JP: – to be unsurprising to people who don't share my point of view.

PM: No, absolutely, and we mustn't expect...I mean I think it's a fundamental thing not to expect answers to questions that you are not addressing. Your concern in *Hope* is total understanding – a theological understanding – so you can't be criticised for not being anchored in the present moment, because that's just part of the –

JP: It's part of the story, but it's not the whole story.

PM: Exactly. But I strongly suspect that many people would prefer Kathryn Tanner's 'realised' eschatology of the present, i.e. belief in a 'present life in God' that is focussed on righting the wrongs of this world. What are your objections to Tanner's eschatology?

JP: I think that 'realised' eschatology – or 'inaugurated' eschatology – is simply saying that what we're thinking about is not a new regime of life beyond death but simply the transforming power of Christ in our present life...that there is a quality to that, which is something human...that that's what it's all about really. And that of course is *easier* to believe than the more mysterious story of truly death and truly resurrection. But it doesn't really do the work, I think, because, OK, our lives are transformed to some extent – perhaps for some of us to a very great extent – in the present during their earthly lives, but that's a temporary phenomenon. And the whole business of resurrection turns on this question of whether the victory of God is one of *everlasting* new life.

PM: Yes, yes. Because, correct me if I'm wrong, but it seems to me that by definition everyone's life is unfulfilled, there is 'unfinished business' in everyone's life.

JP: Yes, I think that is right, yes. There must be more to hope for.

PM: It seems sort of sad and paradoxical, but it has to be so – I would think – because it will be completed later...it will be completed in a different sense!

JP: Let me say a general thing, Patrick. What I was trying to do in *Hope* was to give a defence of the idea – which is counter-intuitive anyway – that there should be a destiny beyond death in which we are recognisably the people we were, not just new people with the old names, and that this makes sense. And I argue that in familiar terms. I argue in the end about the soul, and the nature of the soul. An argument that I think would be as acceptable to a Jew or a Moslem as it is to a Christian. But of course for the Christian there is an *extra* argument, which is the belief in the Resurrection, and that being the seed event from which the whole thing is going to grow. So there's a sort of two-step process, and I've gone to work with those two issues in the book. Whether that's confusing or not, I don't know, but anyway they're there.

PM: Yes. Well, I don't think I'm confused myself –

JP: No I'm not saying *you* are.

PM: But as I say, I suspect that a lot of people don't, in effect, accept that eschatology has to be about the future. It can't be about the present, in the sense that –

JP: Well it has to be about the *meaning* that is to be given to the present by the hope for the future. And Kathryn... You see, this thing arose out of discussion in the Eschatology Project, and scientists who look at these things are very impressed by the *long-term* picture. It's not the only thing, but you know the Weinberg quote about the 'pointlessness' of the universe. And somebody like Kathryn Tanner doesn't seem to be *seized* by that.

PM: No. No. It's just that I feel that many non-theologians – many 'Christians' – are saying to themselves, 'well Christianity is about the present' –

JP: Well of course it is! But it's not *solely* about the present. What it says about the present does not make sense unless there is something in the future.

PM: I accept that, and you say that Tanner's realised eschatology offers a 'healthy corrective to a purely futuristic, "pie in the sky" kind of eschatology'.[16] But I don't think some people have any futuristic view at all. You know, they are confronted with failed politics, famine, economic crisis, environmental disaster, and that's as far as they look. That's their priority, naturally.

JP: Yes, well when Jesus said to the Saducees, 'God is not the God of the dead, but of the living', he was saying, OK, there is an inspiring thing in the story of the patriarchs Abraham, Isaac and Jacob, but it's not the whole story and it's a story that will have continuation and everlasting fulfilment, actually.

PM: Yes. I was re-reading this morning your passages about realised eschatology and you also say – which I thought was very thought-provoking – 'this life is too hurtful and incomplete to be the whole story'.[17]

JP: That's in terms of human terms, but of course it's also true in terms of cosmic terms.

PM: Yes...yes. And you say that Kathryn Tanner's realised eschatology, her 'transcendent present', can at best be only half the story.

JP: Yes. I seem to have said that to you just now!

PM: Yes. Well I accept that. I do. I just feel that lots of Christians would ask of eschatology what it can't give, they're demanding of eschatology something that, by definition, eschatology cannot be.

JP: What is that something, Patrick?

PM: What is the something? Yes. Ethical action... Christianity *lived*... Existential values: belief...love...empathy...as I say, the present.

JP: That's part of the story, but it's not the whole story.

PM: Yes, it's just a contradiction in terms to ask eschatology to be about the present. It's like asking for dry water. One cannot criticise eschatology for not being what it can never be.

JP: Exactly.

PM: On the other hand, you must admit that there's a world of difference between 'lived Christianity' and Barth's Christianity that is 'altogether and entirely eschatology'! What would you say, John, *is* the keystone of the Christian building?

JP: The keystone of the Christian building? It is the belief that God has made a shared human life, thereby making God's nature more clearly known and also by redeeming it. This is the point of St Gregory Nazianzus saying 'what is not shared is not redeemed'. And so God isn't just looking down from heaven and saying 'yes, it'll be all right in the end – I'll give you a golden crown', God is saying, 'yes, I know what it's like'. Gethsemane is a very, very important part of the Christian story. And the cry from the cross 'My God, my God, why have you forsaken me?'. The cry of dereliction is only referred to in Mark and Matthew. Mark gives it in Aramaic, the words that Jesus is alleged to have spoken, and Matthew softens that a little bit by turning it into Hebrew, a more liturgical thing from Psalm 22.

PM: I did not know that. Well I suppose Christians would have their own answers to this. I suppose some would say Christ is the keystone, or love others, love your neighbour is the keystone of Christian belief, but then again that's getting into *presence* rather than *futurity*.

JP: Well, love thy neighbour is obviously – and love your enemy – is obviously an important part of Christ's message, but it isn't the only thing. It's all the things we've just been talking about.

PM: Mm. It seems to me that what gives some non-scientific systems of thought, for example Marxism, Freudianism, or structuralism, their psychological appeal is their ability to explain *everything*; and that, surely, is precisely what's wrong with them. Does Christian eschatology fall into the same category?

JP: No. Christian eschatology is trying to respond to one aspect of what we know about the world, namely that the universe is going to end, either in collapse or decay. And that then raises this question of whether it is all pointless. Christian eschatology was not invented for this particular purpose, but it provides an answer to the question. It says no, it doesn't mean that creation is pointless, it means that for its fulfilment it needs the will of its creator, actually.

PM: I think we've covered this very widely. We've cleared the ground about eschatology, I feel. But would you accept that in *Hope* you have sought to persuade/convert people to Christian eschatology, not to persuade/convert them to Christianity?

JP: Well I would accept that in the following sense. What I tried to do in the book was show that the idea of *any* form of eschatology – human continuation – isn't nonsensical. And that's a very, very important issue. I think that most people themselves feel that, day to day. And then I also wanted to talk about the Christian hope and wanted to indicate that the Christian hope is in my view not just arguing in the dark but there are motivations and meaning to the resurrection of Christ, and that's another aspect of the story.

PM: Yes. I was struck by the fact that early on in *Hope* you yourself acknowledge that

in contemporary Western society, the most immediate threat to religious belief in an ultimately hopeful future is felt to lie not in the longer-term global threats, but in the short-term prospect of certain individual death, together with the widely held view that it results in the annihilation of the person.[18]

JP: I think we are now ready to move onto that?

3

Hope's Seed

Christ's utterances about life after death – The difference between resuscitation and resurrection – Convincing evidence of Christ's resurrection – The Resurrection as continuity/discontinuity – 'God is not the God of the dead' – The soul as 'information-bearing pattern' – God's memory – Gerhard Sauter – The Second Coming – 'Wait and see' – Hope, belief, faith – The Resurrection as the seed of the new creation – The world makes integrated sense.

PM: Would it be true to say that the only *empirical* evidence we have for there being a life after death, for the nature of it, and God's eschatological plan, is the scriptural record of what Christ said about it? Is everything else pure speculation, indeed for Christians 'blasphemous'?

JP: I don't think empirical is quite the word because empirical implies that you can manipulate it, tie it to a board and take measurements, that sort of thing!

PM: Yes. Sorry. I suppose by empirical I mean the written word. The scriptural record of what Christ said about these things is documentary evidence, since he has authority. For instance, I think perhaps the reason a lot of people assume that they or their loved ones go straight to heaven is of course Christ's words on the cross to the penitent thief about being 'in paradise with me today'.

JP: Yes. This is a puzzle. It's well rehearsed in theological circles. I mean 'paradise' is a sort of garden – it's a Persian word meaning 'garden'. So I don't know what the best translation for it would be. I think essentially what Christ is saying is that what is good in you – and your repentance shows there is a seed of that – will not be thrown away.

PM: And of course what strikes everyone is that Christ said the thief will be in paradise and not in hell, despite the thief being a sinner and all the rest of it.

JP: Yes, but 'hell' is a tricky word, because as I said last time the original meant just 'Hades', the abode of the dead, not a place of fire and torment.

PM: But in his lifetime, on this earth, it seems to me that the one consistent thing about Christ's utterances concerning life after death is the phrase 'eternal life'. I mean, we have 'paradise', we have 'many mansions' –

JP: These are all images, if you like, thought-experiments about what it may be like.

PM: Yes. But the most important *concepts* that Christ seems to use are 'eternal life' and 'resurrection'.

JP: Incidentally, about 'many mansions'. That's a poor translation of the Greek. You probably knew that, didn't you?

PM: No, I didn't.

JP: The original word might better be translated as 'caravanserai'. So the picture is not one of a celestial hotel with everything laid on – 'This is your room!' – but of a process.

PM: That's *very* interesting.

JP: So it means there are many 'stages' and all these 'stages' will be open to us. People sometimes say that eternal life would be just boring. You know, sitting on a cloud and shouting hallelujah or something. But it is the unending exploration of the reality of God, progressively unveiled, that seems to me to be behind this image translated in the Authorised Version as 'mansions'. That seems to me the most persuasive picture of the life to come.

PM: We are even more at the mercy of translators than I thought!

JP: Well, these words are exploratory images, they are bound to be difficult to recreate in English.

PM: Another piece of 'empirical' evidence that I think people take from the New Testament as evidence that there is life after death is incidents like the raising of Lazarus, or Jairus's daughter. But I remember when I was a teenager being mystified that there was no record of them describing their after-death experience. If they had really died, and been brought back to life by Christ, where had they been? They never said.

JP: It's very important to have a clear recognition here of the difference between resuscitation and resurrection. Resuscitation is the restoration of THIS sort of life. Lazarus and Jairus's daughter were restored to an active life, but not forever. They were going to die again, and they did. But resurrection is the translation, through death, from this world to another world of reality...the world of the new creation. There has been a lot of interest (it's rather faded again now) in so-called near-death experiences, and it's...there's a sort of...I don't dismiss them altogether, but they *are not* resurrections. They are resuscitations.

PM: But I think there is a lot of confusion in people's minds about it. For instance, the verb 'raise' is used of resurrection from the dead – Christ was 'raised' from the dead – but it is also used of bringing Jairus's daughter back from the dead.

JP: Well I'm not sure that's so, is it? He took her by the hand and called 'arise' and she 'arose straightaway'.[1]

PM: Ah, it's 'rise' in the literal sense, on her bed.

JP: Yes, yes. She was resuscitated.

PM: In the case of Jairus's daughter, Christ says she is 'sleeping', but in Lazarus's case it's stressed that he was dead.

JP: I don't think it's *stressed* that Lazarus is dead, but Jesus takes his state seriously.

PM: I may be too influenced by icons here, which show the people nearest to Lazarus's grave holding their noses, and sometimes even flies buzzing around. But surely, it's made abundantly clear, some might say stressed, that he has been dead for four days? The dictionary definition of resuscitate, I think, is the act of reviving a person from unconsciousness or *apparent* *death*, so if Christ resuscitated Lazarus, was Lazarus really dead?

JP: It's hard to say. The point is, like Jairus's daughter and the son of the widow of Nain, Lazarus was going to die again, he wasn't permanently released from death.

PM: Yet Lazarus is commonly said to have been 'resurrected', isn't he? And I noticed the other day on the Web that Jehovah's Witnesses speak of the 'resurrection' of the widow of Nain's son.

JP: I can't answer for Jehovah's Witnesses, but I do think it's very important to distinguish between resuscitation and resurrection. The son of the widow of Nain died eventually.

PM: If these were resuscitations rather than resurrections, what was Christ intending to prove by them? His *power*?

JP: Certainly he was showing that for God nothing is impossible. But just as important they demonstrate Christ's humanity. He loved Lazarus and his sisters and he was overwhelmed by compassion – he wept. He felt complete solidarity with these humans in their grief, and his resuscitation of Lazarus was the expression of this.

PM: I do think, though, that these examples show how fraught with difficulties it is taking the New Testament texts about life beyond the grave as 'empirical', by which I mean documentary. How easy it is to misread them. It's not surprising if people are confused. I mean, if one assumes that Lazarus, Jairus's daughter and the son of the widow of Nain were *resuscitated*, not resurrected, it explains completely why they didn't have anything to say about their 'after-death experience', or even 'near-death experience', because it is as though they had just been unconscious.

JP: Yes. Or having epileptic fits or in a coma or something. Resurrection is a permanent transition to a new form of life. And it's very important to get that straight.

PM: This is the mystery of Christ's resurrected form, isn't it? That he was *not* just resuscitated.

JP: Absolutely not. Absolutely not, otherwise he would have had to die again. And that would have been the end of the story. So the resurrection is a transition from, if you like, life in the old world to life in the new world. And it's important not to confuse the two.

PM: But the evidence for the resurrection of Christ, I think, is of a completely different order.

JP: Well, obviously, the resurrection of Christ as I understand it, as Christians understand it, is that Christ is the 'first fruits from the dead', the first sign. Whether or not to call *that* empirical is rather a sticky point...I mean the one who wanted the empirical answer was Thomas. Thomas wanted to poke his hands into the wounds, he said 'that's what I've got to do, no nonsense', you know, that sort of thing. But when Christ appeared to him he didn't do that, he just fell at his feet and said, 'My Lord and my God', which is actually the clearest assertion of a divine status of Jesus that you find in the New Testament.

PM: I find that almost unbearably moving.

JP: Yes, well it is. Absolutely. So it's...I mean what we're trying to find is...to steer a path between just saying it's all comforting images and that sort of thing, and that it has to have a reality to it.

PM: I can't remember: did Thomas do *both* the empirical thing and the spiritual thing, as it were?

JP: No, he didn't need to do that. The presence of the risen Lord was enough.

PM: And of course the presence of Christ resurrected was terrifying to the apostles in the first instance.

JP: Yes, it's very interesting that that was the first reaction.

PM: And I find that so authentic.

JP: Yes, absolutely. I mean, something weird is happening here and we wonder: what's going on? It's VERY striking really that the resurrection appearance and the empty tomb, too, are not presented in a triumphalist sort of way in the New Testament at all.

PM: No. But of course when the women encountered Christ resurrected he did tell them not to touch him, didn't he?

JP: Yes. Yes, I don't know how exactly to understand that.

PM: Which implies that it was not a normal physical body.

JP: Well it may also mean just 'don't try and hang onto me'.

PM: Ah yes, 'cling'...yes, yes. 'For I am not yet ascended to my Father.'[2] I have never really understood that 'for'.

JP: Yes, that's mysterious. I think that is a difficult verse. I don't think there would be an agreed interpretation of it.

PM: It is mysterious, isn't it? What I find strangely moving and authentic is that the gospel writers seem to have been so honest about it all. They didn't understand what was going on, it was odd, but they recorded it. They didn't try to explain it away. They even recorded that 'some doubted'.

JP: Yes, they don't make a great song and dance about it really; it isn't a question of an hallelujah chorus and this is the ultimate triumph of everything. When the women found the empty tomb, for example, it's *fear* they experience. And it isn't a question of people saying 'Oh, Jesus – it's nice to see you back again!' and so on. In fact they don't at first recognise him, which is presumably why 'some doubted'. I think the way the stories are presented *is* convincing in the sense that they're not the immediately obvious thing that you might have made up if you just wanted to say 'OK, the message goes on', or something like that.

PM: Yes, yes, it's quite the opposite. It's all so odd that you might have thought they would have skated over it or tried to dress it up or something. But, in a way, you couldn't think it up!

JP: It's sort of matter of fact, in a sense 'this is it, this is what happened'.

PM: Well, I know you have discussed the gospel record of the resurrection in previous books, but I find your account in *Hope* particularly persuasive. In your introduction with Michael Welker to *Ends* you concluded that 'the strongest theme to emerge from all our discussions [...] is the need to wrestle with the necessity for both continuity and discontinuity in any adequate account of eschatology'.[3] This necessity sounds deeply paradoxical, but does the fact that it was difficult to recognise Christ when he was risen *exemplify*, in your view, the continuity / discontinuity in question?

JP: Yes. It also exemplifies, importantly, the difference between resucitation – being made alive again – and resurrection, which is transformation to a new form of life. Somebody like Lazarus came to life again, but it was back to the ordinary life before, when he was going to die in due course. That's not resurrection.

PM: This is something that I did not understand when I was a young man and so concerned with there being no record of Lazarus, or Jairus's daughter, describing their after-death experiences and what they discovered from them. I hadn't really made the distinction.

JP: I think many people don't and I think it's a very important distinction to bear in mind if you're going to make sense of what's going on.

PM: Right. But why is the need to 'wrestle' with this continuity/discontinuity nexus so pressing?

JP: Well if there's going to be true fulfilment, then it can't just be the same old story of this world over and over and over again. On the other hand, it doesn't make sense of the present creation if God simply wipes the slate clean almost thinking 'let's start afresh'. If God is the God of love and faithfulness, Abraham, Isaac and Jacob have to have a future in the divine kingdom. I mean it isn't enough just to make them live again, because then they'll die again. So that's where the discontinuity comes in.

PM: And Christ said that even as he spoke they were living with God, didn't he?

JP: Yes. The Sadducees didn't believe in resurrection and Jesus has his argument with them in Mark 12. He takes them back to Exodus, where God says 'I am that I am and I am the God of Abraham, the God of Isaac, and the God of Jacob', who by then of course were deceased. And Jesus tells the Sadducees, 'God is not the God of the dead, but the God of the living', in other words if the patriarchs really matter to God they are not thrown away.

PM: Yes. It's apodictic really, isn't it? You can't answer that, it's just the final word, really.

JP: Well it's a serious argument.

PM: Why is this continuity/discontinuity relationship so important to a modern eschatology?

JP: It's important because it's saying exactly what Jesus was saying – in the language of his time – that people who matter to God live forever. They are not just packed up and thrown about like broken toys.

PM: To what extent *is* it a discontinuity, then?

JP: There has to be both continuity and discontinuity. I mean it has to be Abraham, Isaac and Jacob who live again in the kingdom of God, not just new characters given the old names for old time's sake, but of course the world of the resurrected is the new creation, it must be different from this world. This world of ours has an inbuilt tendency to decay – the second law of thermodynamics again – so there's not much point in making the patriarchs live again here just to let them die again. They have passed through death into the new creation ('discontinuous'), but they are still the same unique persons ('continuous').

PM: But of course some people might say that the discontinuity is merely one of human apprehension, that if you pass over intellectually from this creation and the world of decay intellectually to the new creation, then the only discontinuity you've made is intellectual. The real person, they might say, is not discontinuous or continuous, but just dead.

JP: No, I think that's exactly the fallacy of failing to recognise that we are essentially embodied beings.

PM: Your discussion in *Hope* of this distinction between animated bodies and incarnated souls was completely new to me.[4] It's so thought-provoking. For instance, when we were at school the passage in Ezekiel – which is so wonderful, so vivid, unforgettable – about the valley of bones, was taught to us as prefiguring the Resurrection. But I read it again last week, and it seems that what you say about the Old Testament view of the soul applies, that these bones are reanimated.

JP: That's right, I think it's about resuscitation rather than resurrection. It's moving in the direction of resurrection, but they didn't get there all in one go.

PM: Well I suppose this is the *beauty* of it, which Pascal brought out when he drew the parallels between the Old Testament and the New Testament and attached such importance to the prophecy and prefiguring of Christ. But I found your discussion of the Old Testament concept very, very interesting. I hadn't thought about this reanimation, this 'animated body' business, before.

JP: Yes, the general Hebrew tendency in the Old Testament was to see people as animated bodies rather than incarnated souls.

PM: Whereas we tend to think the other way round, don't we? That it is not our bodies that are animated but our souls that are embodied.

JP: Well it's 'the real me', and what that is is quite a complicated notion.

PM: Hm...as I understand it, it's difficult to say what the real me is even physically! I mean, I may have got something wrong here, but as I read you in *Hope* most of the atoms in our bodies are replaced every two years?

JP: Yes, that's right.

PM: And yet we look the same, and even our scars and blemishes are the same.

JP: Yes, in my view this a good starting point. We are convinced about the existence of the human person. You're a person, I'm a person, and if that's the case then there must be continuity in you in this world and a continuity in me, and that continuity at first sight appears to be simply material continuance. But that, as I say, is an illusion because in fact the atoms and so on are all changing all the time. And therefore the question is, what is the thing that remains the same, what is the thing that essentially is ME in this world, and which might be the 'me' of the soul – if you like – which God regards as his own? The answer must be, and of course this is hand-waving, because we don't *begin* to understand how to say it exactly, that it's the *pattern* of these things, rather than their mere existence.

PM: Is this analogical to Aristotle's 'form' of the body?

JP: Yes, it's essentially connected with that, yes. And of course Aquinas takes that up too.

PM: So...if this information pattern – which has continuity for physical reasons, neurological reasons, genetic reasons – if it survives into death...what kind of information would it have?

JP: Of itself, it doesn't survive into death. It's a question of the memory of God. If the pattern has a continuance, if it has a significance, it will be held in God's memory. It's a bit like some great picture, a wonderful pattern, a picture. If you burn the picture, you've lost it, it's irrecoverable then. In terms of thinking simply of the material picture, however refined and so forth in a human being, there is no real continuity because in the end it all falls apart. But what I am saying is that a 'pattern' is retained in some way, and I think the best image to use for that – at least, the one most comfortable to me – is of the divine memory.

PM: What do you mean, though, when you say that talk of the soul as the information-bearing pattern is 'hand-waving'?

JP: What I mean by that is that it's beyond our present scientific or philosophical attainments to be able to give an adequate account of the rich complexity of human nature – and of course God's nature too. There are things that we will never be able fully to express. But we have to have some way of talking about them. What I have been trying to do is not to produce a tight theory, it's just to suggest that the *notion* that there is a destiny beyond death is not an *incoherent* notion. It makes sense. I mean many people think, you know, 'a dead body...how can that possibly live again?'. And in terms of bits and pieces, putting the thing together, of course it won't. But it's just to have some way of thinking about it, and I think that's a worthwhile thing to do.

PM: And of course this concept of the information-bearing pattern avoids the evolutionary problem with the soul, doesn't it?

JP: Yes. I mean the soul is not some sort of 'extra spiritual component' injected. Or which evolves at some suitable stage – you know these questions like 'at what stage does the soul arrive in the developing embryo?' and all that sort of thing. Those questions are missing the point.

PM: But how do you conceive of the divine memory?

JP: The divine memory is the perfect recollection of what is there. And that means that God recollects us. God doesn't forget us and so on...so that pattern, though it is dissolved in death, has not disappeared, any more than the fact of my existence has disappeared, in a sort of way. Again, all these things are analogical, but we can't imagine saying that God has somehow 'forgotten' what that chap was like.

PM: Is it a matter of continuance, of continuity, in the sense that he knows us now, he has always known us, and he will continue to know us?

JP: Yes.

PM: I wondered if it's not so much recollection, as knowledge. I don't know...

JP: Well it is retained knowledge, that isn't dissipated. That's what recollection is.

PM: The concept of it is just mind-blowing! I mean, whereas words like 'omniscience' and 'omnipotence' don't cut much ice these days, the idea of the divine memory is just completely...revivifying...

JP: It's very helpful, yes.

PM: Coming back to the discontinuity/continuity nexus, though, I don't really see how the scientific understanding of physical 'process' can corroborate eschatological continuity. To science, surely, death is the end of 'process' – as William Stoeger makes clear in *Ends*, no 'process' is scientifically observable beyond it.

JP: I think modern scientific concepts of process can provide an imaginative resource which can help us discuss what this continuity might be. To take an illustration from physics, we can have *states* that are *continuing*, which are not just frozen in there. And that's what we want. It's very important to accept that there is no *scientific* ground for belief in a destiny beyond death.

PM: No, no.

JP: But equally, if there is no continuity in the discontinuity what is the meaning of it?

PM: And this one resurrection, this unique resurrection in history, Christ's, which was so weird that at first he wasn't recognised, is proof that there *is* continuity beyond the discontinuity of dying?

JP: Yes. I think a lot of – pretty well *all* – the eschatological talk which is not directly concerned with the risen Christ is sort of a thought-experiment. We have no direct experience of what the continuity is going to be like, other than what we learn about the risen Christ.

PM: Although if he returned from the dead, i.e. was resurrected and not resuscitated, surely he would say where he had been and what he had done? You would have thought this would be part of his reassuring message. We are told that after his resurrection Christ 'opened their [the apostles'] understanding, that they might understand the scriptures', but we know very little of what he said.[5] Isn't this all rather strange and unconvincing?

JP: Yes, it's one of the, frankly, mysteries about the New Testament account. Although it says he 'expounded the scriptures' to the two apostles on the way to Emmaus, and told them what it's all about, we don't have a blow for blow, word for word, account for that.[6] It's sort of frustrating, and I'm not exactly sure what to make of it.

PM: And I keep coming back to this fact that he doesn't seem to have said where he has been, and where *they* might be going too. As you say, he has not been resuscitated. If you were resuscitated, like Jairus's daughter and Lazarus, there's nothing you could say.

JP: Well the emphasis in the stories of encounters with the risen Christ is on *Christ*, not on 'OK, you've come back from this strange place with interesting things, tell us what it's all about'. I go back to Thomas, falling on his feet in the presence of the risen Christ rather than actually putting his finger into the print of the nails and thrusting his hand into his side.

PM: Yes. I did once feel that one should forget all this business about him not mentioning where he came back from, as he didn't so much come back from the dead as come back to life and the living. He was back in this world and that is what matters. One could say that it is difficult, therefore, to say what Christ's death proved about the next world, though obvious what it proved about this!

JP: Well, he *manifested* himself in this world and the risen Christ belongs to the new creation, if you like.

PM: Perhaps what he divulged or 'expounded' to the apostles was esoteric, perhaps it was not meant to be for...to go beyond the apostles. So it's not surprising we don't know what he said.

JP: Well no, I don't think that's quite right. I think the apostles are sent out to proclaim to all nations the fact that he was resurrected on the third day and that repentance and forgiveness for sins should be preached in his name.

PM: Yes, the *fact* of his resurrection... In that connection, John, would you mind if I read out this passage from Gerhard Sauter's essay in *Ends*, 'Our Reasons for Hope'? You see, he's very good on this subject, but I found this took a bit of sinking in:

Hope, therefore, is focussed on the resurrection of Jesus Christ. It is the risen Christ who gives us hope. The fact that he is present with us is the source of our hope. Now, we have to be careful, because even this can be mistaken. We may be tempted to say, 'Christ has overcome death, therefore there is hope beyond death even for us.' We have to pay very careful attention to the difference between this sentence and the first one: the *risen* Christ is the one who gives us hope. The risen Christ is the one who claims to be with us now. The fact of his presence is why we can claim to be hopeful.[7]

I don't find I can relate to this, for at least three reasons. First, in what sense do you think Christ is present with us? I mean I believe, I know he is, but he isn't present in his resurrected form, otherwise he would appear to us, and we know he was taken away from us in that form. Also, of course, there is the belief in the second coming.

JP: Yes, well as I said last time, that's a complicated belief which requires more discussion really. I mean, I think of the second coming not as a sudden rending of the heavens and a terrifying judgemental figure appearing, but simply as the assertion that *in the end* God and his Christ are not going to be defeated by death or by the inherent decay of the universe. I think that's the important thing about it.

PM: But I did find myself bridling at this distinction Sauter makes, because... Of course, I thought to myself 'well perhaps I have got this wrong', or 'this is theological rather than experiential', but for me the important thing is the fact of the resurrection in the first place – that that fact gives us so much hope. I don't encounter the resurrected Christ now, I relate to Christ spiritually, so I couldn't understand really why Sauter was so insistent on it being the *risen* Christ who is present with us now, who he says 'claims' to be present with us now, and that it's the fact of his *presence* that gives us hope, not the very fact that he was resurrected.

JP: Well the unrisen Christ wouldn't be much of a sense of hope, would it?

PM: No, I take your point. But it seems to me that if we communicate with Christ, say through prayer, or by asking him as the Truth what we should do about something, that's one thing, and the fact of his resurrection is another. Obviously, we meet him because he *has* been resurrected, but we don't meet him in his resurrected form. This distinction that Sauter makes between the fact of the resurrection and the paramount importance of Christ's presence now, reminds me somewhat of Donne's reference in one of his sermons to 'grammarians': 'Yea, no grammarian can clear it, whether this name Jesus signifie *salvatorem* or *salutem*, the instrument that saves us, or the salvation that is afforded us; for it is not only his person, but his very righteousness that saves us.'[8] Sauter is hair-splitting, isn't he?

JP: Well possibly. I would say Christ is the means of our salvation. We don't swallow that salvation up in some sort of a Christ-figure, we retain our individualities. That's what is the value to God and value to us of course, and this is where we are back to the continuity / discontinuity theme.

PM: Do you think it's impossible, really, to speculate how we communicate with Christ?

JP: Yes, yes, I think it's...if you want it all spelled out, that's just too pedestrian to encompass. I mean, there is a mystery here. It's very important in theology not to lose the concept of mystery, but equally not to overplay the mystery card and say 'well, we can't understand that, but don't worry, it's all right'. So of course there is a mystery, and the answer to many of these eschatological queries is 'wait and see'.

PM: Ha, well I agree with you there, I absolutely agree with you! I wasn't happy either with Sauter's idea that Christ 'claims' to be with us now, or even his use of 'hope'. Why should we be 'tempted' to say 'Christ has overcome death, therefore there is hope beyond death even for us'? Surely, if Christ was resurrected, there certainly is hope for us beyond death, in fact it's not just a hope but a certainty, isn't it, assuming we accept that Christ's human nature was the same as ours? We can *believe* there is life after death. I was struck by how many contributions there are in the second half of *Ends* about hope and the significance of hope, rather than faith or belief.

JP: Well, as Fraser Watts says in his contribution, 'there is probably no more religious emotion than hope'.[9]

PM: Do you believe that hope is part of man's true nature, really? Is it innate?

JP: I think most people have a sort of intuition of hope that in the end it does make sense, that in the end 'all shall be well, and all manner of things shall be well' as Julian of Norwich says. The question is: where can such an intuition find its basis? What I'm saying, of course, is in the love and faithfulness of God, but then we also have to ask 'how can we make *sense* of that thing?', and that poses exactly the continuity / discontinuity question.

PM: But what is the difference between hope and faith? Surely Christians don't just hope, they believe, they have faith?

JP: Well, let's just think about hope for a minute. We use 'hope' in two senses. One is a rather feeble sense of just expressing a wish: 'I hope this marrow will win the prize', that sort of thing. Or: 'I hope it will be a fine day tomorrow for the cricket match.' That's a wish-list use of hope. What one's interested in, I think, is a stronger thing than that, that what is desirable in that sense will be brought about by some influence which is reliable – which we can trust to bring it about. And I think that can only mean God, in some clear sense. And the question then is 'does that make sense?', or... If it's just a question of God wiping the slate clean and saying 'let's see if we can do better next time', that doesn't make much theological sense I think.

PM: Of course, I agree with you. Do you think though that that kind of hope really at some point becomes faith?

JP: Well, hope is...hope certainly...hope and faith are connected. As I say, hope is the trust that there is, in this case, a God who can bring about a fulfilment. And that trust is itself faith, it is the commitment. Faith is not just a question of abstract knowledge...it is important, a personal commitment, and trust in things. I mean, I believe there are mountains on the moon, but that doesn't affect me in any particular way. But if faith is really trust dependent on the good will of a creator, it's something that will affect my life. I can't believe that Jesus was the son of God and was raised from the dead without it affecting my life. It isn't just a question of ticking the boxes, it is a question of how you orient your whole existence.

PM: Is there a sense in which theology is less...fideistic...less faith-driven today? And more tentative? More *hopeful*, simply?

JP: Well it depends what you mean by fideistic. I mean 'fideistic' usually is used as rather a term of reproach, and it involves believing in some infallible source of information that gives you the answer to everything – the Bible, of course, traditionally has played that role. I think the Bible is something much more subtle than that. It isn't a question of 'this is the textbook in which you look up all the answers', it is a question of the story of unfolding interaction with humankind and the motivation therefore for our trust in that.

PM: There is a character in a story by Chekhov – *The Duel*. And this character is arguing with a scientist about belief. The scientist passionately believes in 'Darwinism', or vulgar Darwinism at least. The word for 'belief' is the same in Russian as 'faith'. And the other character says, 'I have an uncle who is a village priest. When the peasants ask him to come and pray for rain during a drought, he takes his umbrella and a mackintosh with him, so that he won't get wet on the way home!'

JP: Ha!

PM: 'That is faith!' he says.

JP: Yes, well as I say, faith involves commitment. It's not just a wish-list, 'it would be really nice if I won the lottery' or whatever it might be.

PM: But I *believe* Christ was resurrected because of the evidence. I don't need to have *faith* in that.

JP: Well I think you can't have faith without belief. You can't commit yourself to something you don't think is a reality, and so I think that the difference between faith and belief is that faith involves a *commitment*. I believe there are mountains on the moon but so what? I mean, it's an interesting fact but it doesn't carry things any further. But I can't believe that Jesus was raised from the dead without consequences for my own life and my thoughts about others.

PM: So would I be right in saying that you *believe* that Jesus was raised from the dead because of the evidence?

JP: Well of course belief has to be motivated. I don't think belief is just shutting your eyes and gritting your teeth. That's coming back to our weak sense of 'hope'. But equally I don't think you can believe that Christ was raised from the dead without it affecting your life. As I say, it isn't just the satisfaction of a curiosity.

PM: Do you think we *believe* in the faithfulness of God, or do we have *faith* in it? Or do we, as contributors to *Ends* seem more inclined to say, *hope* for it?

JP: I believe we have *grounds* for believing in the faithfulness of God and when we fully commit ourselves to that, that is faith rather than just belief. As I said, faith is not merely belief in the sense of x is true or y is true, it is that the truth of x and y is something that influences and changes my life.

PM: So would you say that you have belief in the end of the universe but faith in the new creation?

JP: Yes, I would! Yes. Yes. We are back where we've been many times in this conversation, Patrick. To have a hope of a destiny beyond death is an indirect assertion of a belief in one who brings that about, who is faithful. I think many people have a true and lasting hope. Really true and lasting hope is not just a question of whistling in the dark for a while, it can only have its basis and its guarantee in the faithfulness of God, really.

PM: But we seem to agree – to believe – that in Sauter's words 'hope is focussed on the resurrection of Jesus Christ'. Not just in terms of our survival beyond death, which you said at the end of our previous conversation was the most pressing question in contemporary western society, but in terms of making sense of the 'longer-term global threats' and the death of the universe.

JP: Yes. We talk about the Resurrection as the seminal event. I mean the Resurrection *is* the seminal event. It is literally the seed from which so much grows in Christian eschatology, just as Christ said in John 12 that if a grain of wheat 'dies' in the ground it 'brings forth much fruit', and St Paul in I Corinthians 15 that seed is 'not quickened except it die'. The Resurrection is seminal in a very deep sense. In a sense that the afterlife – as far as I can understand anyway – the ultimate destiny of creation is to be fulfilled by the old creation, which we know, being transformed into the new creation, which we don't yet know. That is the continuity / discontinuity of it.

PM: The new creation is born from the old, '*ex vetere*'...

JP: *Ex vetere*, exactly. And, of course, the resurrection of Christ is the 'seed' event – the seminal fact – from which that new creation has already begun to grow. At the moment, they exist, in some sense, alongside each other. So in the end the destiny of one is to be transformed into the other.

PM: Coming back to what you have said is Western society's most pressing anxiety, however – survival after death – it seems to me that in *Hope* you do *not* argue that after death we shall immediately go to a new life in the spirit, you offer people the certainty of resurrection at some indeterminate point in their future. For instance, you write that the chapters 'Personhood and the Soul' and 'The New Creation' together 'set out the form of human hope as being death and resurrection, rather than some kind of spiritual survival', and later that 'there is indeed the Christian hope of a destiny beyond death, but it resides not in the presumed immortality of a spiritual soul, but in the divinely guaranteed eschatological sequence of death and resurrection'.[10] Have I understood you correctly here? If I have, don't you think a lot of people concerned about a personal life after death will be disappointed to learn that it will be only 'some form of re-embodiment'?[11]

JP: Well, what do you mean by 'immediately' go to a new life? We're thinking of the time of this world, and it's difficult to know how that relates to the time of the world to come. As I say, we might all arrive at the resurrection point at the same time, but it's not the time of this world. I think it's important that the hope of ourselves is of a true, human survival and that we are not spiritual beings – ghostly beings – who happen to have a body at the moment but that's a thing to get rid of. There's a lot of thinking along those lines, of course – 'creatures of the flesh' and so on – but I think it's important, absolutely intrinsic, to human beings that we are this strange sort of mixture of the spiritual and the material. Therefore if *we*, as ourselves – not as some sort of recollections or symbols or something – are going to survive, it must involve a bodily existence of some kind.

PM: But when we actually die, do you believe we go to Christ? St Paul seems to say that we shall be with Christ immediately after we die.[12] Are we then with Christ?

JP: Yes, I think we are. I think we are always with Christ in this world too, but then we shall be in a more manifest way. We will know *him*, and we will know ourselves, as he knows us, which is part of what the process of creation is about.

PM: And will we know God?

JP: Well yes! The point, however, is of course that God infinite is not fully known by human beings and Jesus is the incarnate image of God. What is true of him is true of God and he is our access to God, in that sense.

PM: The reason I ask this question is that when I was in Italy recently I picked up a newspaper and it had an interview in it with Cardinal Camillo Ruini about his new book, which Benedict XVI had asked him to write, entitled *C'è un dopo? (Is There an Afterlife?)*, and the journalist asked him: 'On the last day, where will we be? You cite St Paul, according to whom we will be "with Christ" immediately after we die. But how will we be?' Ruini's answer was simply: 'We shall be with Christ, and with God the Father, in so far as we will participate in all of their life, we shall be known and loved by them, and in our turn we will know and love them.'[13]

JP: I think that's a very good answer, but you have to understand the answer, I think, in terms of a process rather than a 'gee whizz' moment.

PM: Yes... What Ruini adds is: 'not as at present in the light and dark of faith, but we will know them directly in their sublime reality'.

JP: Well, yes. But as I say, that knowing is a process, it isn't that you're suddenly injected with the thing.

PM: Connected with this, I agree with you in *Hope* that the urgent question for most people is whether they will see their loved ones again. Your own reply is: 'Yes – nothing of good will be lost in the Lord.' But isn't this a *non sequitur*? I agree that nothing of good could be lost in the Lord, but that's not the same as *seeing* your loved ones again. And might not your reply strike people as particularly illogical given that you appear to *reject* 'some kind of spiritual survival' after the death-event in favour of resurrection at some indeterminate future point?

JP: Well I think it's not a question of *seeing* our loved ones again, it's the restoration – or *continuation* – of a relationship that you had with them. There will be some persisting relationship and that is a good. I mean I think one of the greatest goods of life in this world is our relationship to those who are near and dear to us, and that is a good that will not be lost I think. It will be renewed and continued.

PM: In the spirit?

JP: Well, as human beings. And if we have to be embodied as human beings, as I believe we have, then it will involve that. It will involve that. I mean, human relationships in this world are more than merely fleshly – they have a different dimension to them.

PM: Let's return to our core subject, the real focus of our conversation, which is the truth of Christ's resurrection. Does belief in Christ's resurrection, and therefore our resurrection, AUTOMATICALLY entail belief in the Christian eschatological scheme? If we believe that Christ was raised from the dead, does that automatically entail an eschatological scheme for creation, for the universe?

JP: Well, I've been trying to say to you...the question all the time is to what degree does the world make integrated sense or not? And if the order and fruitfulness of the world is a reflection of God's will for it, then it must be not just a transient, fortunate piece of fruitfulness – now appearing, now lost – but the whole show must be an integrated and meaningful thing, it seems to me.

PM: I accept that. But it says on the blurb of *Hope* 'science tells us that the universe will end in cosmic collapse or decay. If this is so, can there be credible hope of personal existence after death?' and I don't think everyone would accept the logical / causal connection between these two statements. People with their chopping logic say things like 'why should the fact that the universe will end PRECLUDE a personal destiny after death?'.

JP: Well it doesn't, strictly. The question is, if we're looking for a theological understanding of the world, it has to be a total and all-embracing understanding. It isn't a question of picking out the bits and pieces that make sense. And the continuity / discontinuity of Christ's resurrection, which we seem in complete agreement about, opens out into that.

PM: Yes. The...destiny of an eschatology derived from Christ's resurrection appears to be the 'new creation'. Does anything come *after* this new creation, or is that the teleological 'end', a kind of Utopia attained once and for all?

JP: When you ask to what extent there's a teleological 'end', you make it sound like a sort of winning-post...and once you've got there, 'we made it'!

PM: Well, it's the *telos*; you know – 'end', 'purpose'...

JP: Yes, exactly, but the new creation is not a static world, it's an unfolding world, as I say, of exploration into the increasingly revealed, deep reality of God. God has a purpose, I think, for all creatures. Not just for humankind, but a purpose which is appropriate for people.

PM: Yes. I agree. The problem, I think, that a lot of people have is reconciling in their minds the idea of the new creation, or let's say the New Jerusalem, with their own resurrection because they think of resurrection as too physical, too bodily, too much like resuscitation, in fact.

JP: It's a body, it's a body. It's not physical in the sense of the body in matter, the character of this world. As I say, it's not a static world, it's a world of unfolding life.

PM: Yes. Well you can see where I was going. I was suggesting that perhaps a lot of people would regard the new creation as a kind of utopia, and utopia has been –

JP: Well in one sense, if you are thinking of it as a sort of high-class hotel, with champagne cocktails for free, if that's your picture of utopia, it's not that.

PM: I think the essential feature of utopias, for me, having experienced the Soviet Union, for instance, and reading Plato or Thomas More, is that 'it's always like this', it's an achieved state of stasis, 'the end'. For instance, in the late 1960s I visited a collective farm in the USSR and a man who was growing cucumbers explained Marxism-Leninism to me. First, he said, there was capitalism in Russia, now they were living under socialism, and after that would come communism. When I asked him what would come after communism, he simply said 'nothing'. If people think the new creation is some kind of 'state' or 'stasis', that is terrible, really. But I think we've all been affected by Platonic, or other, notions of the future.

JP: Well absolutely. I mean the Platonic tradition says that the height of reality is stasis. There's some 'peak', where whichever direction you move in is going to be diminishing. But the new creation is a *dynamic* perfection rather than a static perfection.

PM: I welcome this, of course. That is most interesting, most interesting. And it's so different from *philosophical* notions of a noetic world, or world of forms, or philosophical notions of 'perfection'.

JP: As I say, we have to rid ourselves of the notions of perfection as a high point from which no movement is possible. We should think of the new creation as entering into the most open reality – endlessly developing.

PM: But do you think most people believe they will go straight to heaven when they die, or at least straight to the presence of their loved ones?

JP: This is a long-debated question and there's been no theological agreement upon it. In Reformation times there was a frequent feeling that there must be what is called 'soul sleep' – a sort of anaesthetised period of waiting for the actual resurrection. I think the answer to that is, as to so many eschatological questions, 'wait and see'.

PM: Well actually that's my answer to everything in this area! Although you say in the introduction to *Hope* that you are not setting out to 'prove' Christian eschatology, you display tremendous courage in invoking reason and science to 'present the motivations for Christian eschatological hope', as you put it.[14] But what would you say to a reader who concluded that life after death and the new creation are *not* susceptible to reason because you yourself repeatedly fall back on 'the faithfulness of God' and 'wait and see'?

JP: It comes back to what we were saying last time – this idea of 'thought-experiments'. I think *all* our eschatological talk is exploratory thinking. And I say 'wait and see' simply because if the outcome of the fulfilment of the whole thing is this endless exploration of the reality of God, that's not something we'll be able to imagine beforehand. It will exceed our expectations.

PM: As I say, I think you show great courage in addressing these questions. If I try to trace back to when I was a child my own thoughts and feelings about 'heaven' or the life beyond, and those of other people around me, I feel now that there was an unresolved distance in people's minds between the immediate after-death experience and their resurrection. I feel that a lot of people I knew – who were Christians – couldn't really connect the two, as it were. They believed in an *immediate* further existence, an immediate life let's say with God, in the spirit, but they couldn't tie that in with resurrection, except through the dramatic 'exploratory' images of the somewhat confusing apocalypses of the New Testament.

JP: I don't know quite what to say about that. But what I do think is that actually a fundamental Christian understanding (though it has often got lost in discussion down the ages) is that we are embodied beings by our very nature, and therefore if we have a true existence beyond death it's not as some sort of apprentice angels or something like that, it has to be an 'embodied' belief, and that's why I think resurrection, as exemplified by the resurrection of Jesus Christ, is so much more credible than these vague ideas of spiritual survival and so on.

4
Death Is Real

Jesus really died – The fear of annihilation – Bereavement – Secularisation of remembrance – Popular animistic beliefs – The 'second presence' of the dead – Modern concern with 'closure' – Dylan Thomas – Death as the ultimate trusting in God's faithfulness – But we fear the act of dying – Christ's agony in the Garden – The 'cry of dereliction' – Death as grave and gateway.

PM: What *is* death? We spoke earlier about William Stoeger's reference in *Ends* to the 'scientific description of death', but what is it philosophically, theologically? There's 'clinical' death, 'brain death', 'resuscitation', 'near-death experiences', but what is *death*?

JP: I think strictly we want to avoid medical definitions of these things, but I would say that it's something like this: it is the *irreversible* cessation of the processes that keep the body working. And the important thing is to stress the irreversibility of it. I think it's intrinsic to death that that's what it is about. There's no *natural* reversal of a person's death.

PM: So are you saying Christ reversed an irreversible process by a miracle?

JP: Well I say, first, that Christ truly died. It's very important that Jesus really died. Christianity has always understood that the Word became flesh in order to *share* and thereby redeem all human experience, and that includes the experience of death. So it isn't a question that Jesus sort of slides by that. Holy Saturday is a neglected part of Passion Week. It's not just the time for getting the Easter flowers ready in the church, it's deeply integral to the meaning of Easter. And it's important that the Bible doesn't talk about Jesus resurrecting himself, it always says 'he was raised from the dead' – and in Romans 8 it says that it took place by the work of the Holy Spirit, so it's God's work but not that of the second person of the Trinity, Christ himself. Christianity has always taken death seriously. It doesn't think it's, you know, going into the next room, or that sort of thing, Death is REAL. It looks final.

PM: Yes, when it's happened and you are left with an unalive body, it does.

JP: But it's not the ultimate reality. Because only God is ultimate. But if there is a destiny beyond death, then that will not result from some clever manipulation of things exactly as they are, but must be some new action...act of God. It's interesting indeed that the Creed, for example, takes the death of Jesus seriously – he really did die. 'He descended into Hell', or Hades, as it should be. So again, it isn't that, as people sometimes suggest, he recovered in the cool of the tomb and that sort of thing. Death was a real end but, as I say, not the ultimate end because only God is ultimate.

PM: Yes. Why do you think we fear death so much? Is it the *state* of death as we imagine it (which of course we can't), or the fact of leaving this beautiful world, or the possible agony of dying?

JP: I don't know. There are a variety of reasons. But I think what we really fear is annihilation.

PM: Is that fear really a very strong will to *live*?

JP: Yes. A will to persist as a person. Not to just be wiped off the slate.

PM: Do you feel most people experience that very strong will to live beyond death and all they need is proof that it continues?

JP: Not quite. We can't prove it. As I say, I think a destiny beyond death only becomes intelligible with a picture of reality where physical processes are not the whole story. Death is ultimate within the physical process, but only God is truly ultimate.

PM: Well, whatever we believe about life beyond death, those who are left behind grieve.

JP: Of course.

PM: And find it extremely difficult, and sometimes they say they never get over it.

JP: Yes. In terms of this life, death is a real separation. And...I often think of...suppose you were in the nineteenth century and a very close member of the family was going off to Australia. And you would never see them again. They wouldn't die, necessarily, but they... Separation is real, and as I say, it's very important that Christianity, in my view, takes death *seriously*. It doesn't say, 'it's nothing to worry about' sort of thing, it says 'there is hope beyond death, because there is one who is beyond death himself', which is God.

PM: Yes...yes. Some people have asked me 'why does God put us through this?', when they have lost a loved one. Well, you know, hehhh, it's very difficult to answer that.

JP: We live in a world which is not totally stable and this developing comes at a cost... We have good reason to think that only a world in which, so to speak, things change – and really change – is a world which would evolve new things. So I think it's the 'shadow side', if you like, of the fruitfulness of the world, the world of creation as it's been established; and that's just inevitable.

PM: I found the German Protestant Jürgen Moltmann's article in *Ends*, 'Is There Life after Death?', very powerful, but he says something on this theme that I don't think I agree with him about. He says that in modern society 'we can observe a quite unusual suppression of the awareness of death and the remembrance of the dead'.[1]

JP: Well I think I do agree with him. You see, if there is no hope of a destiny beyond death given to us by a faithful God, death really is the end, it's annihilation, and that's how many people think about it. There is a very great reluctance in a lot of society to talk frankly about death. It's treated as the absolute worst thing that can happen to you.

PM: Ha! Well I suppose most people do think that and, as I say, it has a devastating effect on those nearest to you. We all know you never get over it really, in your loved ones, the closest ones to you. On the other hand, you see, I am struck by the way that people in recent years – the last twenty years, say – have been creating shrines everywhere to the dead. You know, if there is a traffic accident, or someone has a fatal heart attack, that spot becomes a shrine, which is maintained over the years with flowers etcetera. It only needs a crucifix or a Madonna to resemble a roadside shrine in Italy or Poland...

JP: I think that's partly to do with the feeling that that's the best thing you can do.

PM: Surely. And people seem much more concerned with the anniversaries of death. The lengths that some families go to now, to return to where their loved one died or is buried, surprise me. Long plane journeys or train journeys or ferries every year, on anniversaries. I just feel there is a school of thought that says the remembrance of the dead isn't suppressed, it has become more paganised.

JP: Yes, I think that's probably true.

PM: On the other hand, we know from surveys in the last decade or so, that around 60% of the population in Britain and Germany believe in a higher being and some form of life after death; and everyone is surprised by this figure.

JP: Yes, I am surprised by it, certainly.

PM: Of course, it makes no reference to Christianity, or going to a church. So do you think, perhaps, that the surge in secular commemoration of the dead has something to do with the 'hospitalisation' of dying, the clinicalisation of death in western societies?

JP: Yes, I do. Because death is thought of as a frightful thing there is a tendency to shut it away. Equally, because of the general reluctance to acknowledge the reality of death people themselves feel they must be shut away and not intruding. I mean, if you think about a dinner party, all sorts of things might be talked about, but I'm willing to bet that the least likely thing is the nature of death!

PM: Mmm. I have to say that in my experience I encounter awareness of death everywhere. The other day I went into our butcher's shop and a butcher whom I don't really know (he's not the main man) started talking to me about his father's death, which the family obviously knew was imminent. I don't know him at all! He was talking to me, so I said certain things and what have you, and then he amazed me by saying: 'Thank you and God bless you.' I don't think people *are* unaware of death. It's now even shown on television, of course.

JP: I think there is a little bit of a taboo about talking about death. I still think a dinner party would go fairly quiet if somehow that issue were raised seriously.

PM: You have never done that have you, John?

JP: No I haven't.

PM: Ha! Nor have I!

JP: I think it would be unhelpful, to throw it in their face just like that, so to speak.

PM: Yes. But can I mention to you some experiences that people have described to me after the death of loved ones? I think it's quite common for the bereaved to identify the deceased with living *creatures* that seem to just turn up, for instance cats, birds, butterflies, or a dragonfly.

JP: Well I've never heard of that. I've never encountered this phenomenon.

PM: A lady in my home town was widowed and told me that a male blackbird had suddenly turned up in her garden, was very tame, and she felt a close relationship with it, till it just as suddenly disappeared. A greengrocer was widowed, he kept working before his wife's funeral, and one sunny afternoon a large dragonfly flew into the shop, settled on his chest, then flew out again. Another person told me of two barn owls perching on their mother's coffin as it stood in the garden. And several people have described to me butterflies that have suddenly appeared. I wouldn't like to say how these people read this phenomenon, but they definitely feel an association...the appearance of these creatures has somehow comforted them – reassured them.

JP: Well I think these are sort of devices to try and deconstruct death a bit.

PM: Certainly. Certainly.

JP: And I wouldn't want to be *harsh* about them and say these were stupid...

PM: No, as it happens the lady and the grocer were lifelong Christians, but it just interested me that this almost animistic belief could exist. What's going on here, in your opinion? Is it 'paganism'? I think an awful lot of people do have these experiences, *pace* Moltmann.

JP: This is a new thought for me. Of course people are bruised by the death of others and they seek what amelioration they can. What I think is important is to try and do so on an honest basis.

PM: Supremely important, isn't it, supremely important. What do you make then of people saying that they feel a presence...the 'presence' of the departed? I think Moltmann is very good here. He writes in *Ends*:

Once we understand their death not as a farewell but as their transformation into that other world of God's and that other life which we call eternal life, we experience their presence in our life as a kind of 'second presence'. In this strange 'second presence' the dead do not bind the living to themselves but let them go free, although the living know that they are still bound to those who are gone. That is why the survivors do not have to forget the dead in order to be able to lead their own lives.[2]

JP: Lots of people do feel that and if you have any pastoral care in a parish you'll encounter people who will tell you so. I've always wanted to be very careful in how I respond to that. I didn't want to say to them 'no, I don't think that's right' and so forth.

PM: Mmm. For me it's not just a form of 'recollecting' the dead, which is why I have always had doubts about that passage in Kierkegaard where he says one should be 'very careful about poetically conjuring up the dead' because 'the most dreadful thing is just this, that one who is dead gives no hint of anything at all'.[3] Unfortunately, I suppose that from 'second presence' to spiritualist seance can be just a small step, can't it?

JP: Yes. Well this is a very painful and difficult area. It's very easy for some to manipulate people, sometimes with good intentions to ameliorate the situation, and I think the only answer in the end is to try and face reality as it is in its puzzling – and I think not unhopeful – way.

PM: Thank you, John. And of course there *is* a modern tendency to think that we must have 'closure' on everything –

JP: Yes.

PM: – and that 'closure' equals 'oblivion'.

JP: Well the resurrection is the opposite of closure, it's the *opening*, if you like, of new possibilities.

PM: Yes, I feel the same. I have never really understood this 'closure' thing. My own experience, over time, of the death of those near to me has been Moltmann's 'second presence'.

JP: Yes, absolutely.

PM: I always feel they are not remote. Of course you are devastated by their physical absence, of course you are, and the trauma is never far away. But I think 'second presence' is a very apt description of how they live on with you. In actual fact, do you believe that there *can* be purely psychotherapeutic closure after a loved one's death? Is it even desirable?

JP: I'm not sure exactly what you mean by that.

PM: Well, of course I recognise that we all need therapy – tenderness and care – after the death of a loved one, but what is 'closure' on it? Can psychotherapy alone bring relief? Why should we expect their death to be 'closed off' from us, is that right, or the best thing for us?

JP: But it doesn't mean 'forget about it, don't worry about it', it's coming to terms with it. I mean, that's the problem we have throughout life – coming to terms with reality or whatever. For example, coming to terms with the fact that you might be actually totally disabled.

PM: Yes...and it's a process. It should be a process, shouldn't it, rather than some sort of target you must achieve? I'm referring to the way that 'closure' is used today, rather glibly, I think.

JP: I think it is, I think it is. But closure is quite often, I think, used about people, the circumstances of whose death or even the actuality of whose death, are not clear to those near them, and closure comes from knowing what happened.

PM: That is a very important point. Yes. You tend to get counsellors using the word 'closure' as though everyone needs it, but I think you're right, there's a special class of people who have open questions about a death, who don't know enough about the circumstances or something, particularly murders and disappearances, and they desperately need to know the facts *before* they can begin the process of grieving... It's 'closure' on the event, rather than on their grieving.

JP: And, of course, even believers may need a long time to come to terms.

PM: Yes, this is no 'glib' kind of closure...

JP: Death is a real separation – and that is costly – but it's not a separation forever.

PM: No, no. Do you think then that in this case psychotherapists are largely trying to comfort people who are without belief, or whose beliefs are secular?

JP: Well I can't comment on what they're aiming for, but I think an important part of the process must be – as I say – to face reality, to not live in a fantasy world.

PM: Yes. I often feel that with 'closure' some sort of fantasy consolation is being concocted and that it's really a bit of a con-trick.

JP: I think that could be so.

PM: Another difficult question, I think, which I have come across in Edwardian letters that I am working with at the moment, is when people doubt or reject their faith, or the comfort of faith, *in extremis*, on their death bed. Do you think this happened more in the past?

JP: I think people feel the notion – sometimes I feel it myself, actually – that...the idea of there being a destiny beyond death is too good to be true.

PM: I hadn't thought of that.

JP: People are terribly wary. They don't want to kid themselves.

PM: Yes, yes. The only experience I have had of it, in a way, was with my mother, actually, who had always been a strong believer and a member of the Church of England. I'd been caring for her for some years, but when it came to the moment I was delayed in getting to her – through mistakes at the hospital, unfortunately – but I still got to her, and when she was very distraught, as I think she realised what might happen, I did try to comfort her, in a Christian way, holding her hand and speaking into her ear because she was half-conscious. She knew who I was and she reacted to what I said, but I think her mind was so concentrated... I think when people come to dying – I've seen this with animals – their mind is so concentrated on what is happening –

JP: Right.

PM: – and what *is*, and the fact that they are going – that everything else seems an irrelevant distraction. That's the feeling I had, that she didn't need me to talk about this. You know?

JP: Again you have to be sensitive about these things and the last thing to do is to bounce in and say 'don't worry, it's all right!'.

PM: Yes. What did you, as a vicar, say to people who asked you what happens after we die?

JP: A crude but not altogether lacking-in-truth answer would be to say 'wait and see'.

PM: But of course they asked you because they thought you know more than that!

JP: Well somehow or other I often pray to make a good death when my time comes. And part of being a good death, I think, is to commit oneself into the hands of a faithful creator and merciful saviour as the liturgy says, and I think that's what it is: we enter the presence of God in some way. Exactly how that happens, we don't know. One thing I do think is that God does not work by magic, ever. There's always some sort of process, so there will be an entering into the life of God in a new and much more profound way, so in a sense there's something to look forward to, but of course the painful side of death is the separation side of it –

PM: Yes.

JP: – and in my view that is only a temporary difficulty.

PM: So you don't believe in 'Rage, rage against the dying of the light'? I don't really understand that poem of Dylan Thomas's – 'Do not go gentle into that good night'. It has become very famous, of course, and is often quoted approvingly, as a kind of secular/humanist poem for our age. Although he has the line 'Though wise men at their end know dark is right', and the night is repeatedly described as 'good', the overwhelming meaning seems to be that there is no other life but this one and we should fight even in death to hang onto it.

JP: Yes, well I think the poem – it's a very powerful poem, of course – I think it portrays exactly the situation of somebody who believes there *is* no destiny beyond death, so there really is a black night that you just disappear into, and he wants to face that, wants his father to face that, with a somewhat heroic defiance, which I think one has to admire to some extent, but which is not the whole story. So what this poem is illustrating, I think, from the point of view of our discussion, is the really 'blank' nature of the world, the fact that, despite its fruitfulness, if there is no continuation, no destiny beyond death for human beings, or deeper universe itself, then the world has a foolish aspect. That's how I read the poem.

PM: Yes, it seems a kind of Promethean shout, or Sisyphean protest, which, as you say, is very powerful... But do you think the claim is philosophically defensible that there is only one world – this world?

JP: Well, I don't believe there is, because there is the world of God's new creation, which is not fully in existence now, but the point is: if we simply take – seriously, as we should – what science tells us, then there *is* only one world and we are, if you like, *trapped* in it. I mean, there is nowhere else to go! And I think this poem illustrates the sort of frustration and the feeling that the whole thing doesn't make sense in the end if that's the position you hold. But the point is: there is a greater reality than the reality of the process of this world, and that is the will and purpose and power of a benevolent creator. And it's through him that there is a destiny beyond death. I think there's no other *credible* basis that I'm aware of for such a belief, other than there being, as I say, a creator who is both faithful and powerful.

PM: I find the poem's rhetoric quite...unstable, but it seems to be based on a kind of, well, at most positivist view of life that we only have this life and so we must add our farthing to it. We must do our thing for it to the bitter end.

JP: That's exactly what the poem is about. It is saying, you know, 'defy that' (death). I mean, it's not sensible. 'Defy' doesn't mean you stop death occurring to you –

PM: And why should one fight to hang onto this life if one is manifestly designed to leave it?

JP: Well, we're not manifestly *designed* to leave the world, but we cannot help leaving it! If we say 'designed to leave the world' that is putting purpose into it, and unless there is a fulfilment, a continuation of you and me beyond death, that purpose seems highly questionable to say the least.

PM: Yes....yes...it's certainly a challenging poem. I think it is a far more challenging poem than many people realise. This morning, for instance, I looked on the Web for discussions of this poem and what you and I have been saying is totally missing.

JP: What is in its place?

PM: 'Fight to the last gasp'; an intrinsic value in *denying* death, really.

JP: Well that's the sort of feeling that leads to this modern tendency of excessive medical intervention. As if death was the worst thing that can happen to you and therefore if you postpone it for even a day you've achieved something.

PM: So do you incline more really to the medieval view of *Ars Moriendi*, the 'art of dying'?

JP: Yes, absolutely. Death itself, I think, is the ultimate trusting...putting oneself in the hands of God and trusting in God's faithfulness.

PM: Is it true to say, then, that Christian believers are not afraid of death?

JP: I think the answer is yes and no about that. I mean, as a Christian I do not believe that death is an 'end'. Nevertheless, I don't think like Peter Pan that to die will be just a great adventure. Jesus's agony in the Garden of Gethsemane shows us that he took death seriously, if I may say that. So, we should take it seriously. But, as I say, taking it seriously in conjunction with a belief in a faithful creator and a merciful saviour.

PM: Yes. I find the semantics of the English words 'death', 'dying', 'died', 'dead', rather confusing. You know, you have this verb with its preterite and past participle 'died', but you also have this adjective 'dead', and then 'death' can be used as an abstract noun meaning 'the state of having died/being dead', and colloquially as a verbal noun meaning 'the action of dying'. I would actually propose using 'death' as the state or concept of being dead, and 'dying' for the action, as it were. And it seems to me that it is slightly easier to talk about death as a state or as a life beyond than it is about *dying*. For instance, you are not afraid of death – indeed, of course, you believe in the life beyond that moment – but are you afraid of dying?

JP: Well I think that's... I think that we *are* afraid of dying. The modern ideal for death, I think, is to go to sleep at night and your relations come in and find you dead in the morning: no long struggle. And that struggle...it *is* a struggle. And that is why we have to be careful about palliative medicine that keeps us going for too long. A lot of understanding of the Christian attitude to death must centre on the story of Gethsemane: Jesus was facing the prospect of an extremely painful and long drawn out death and he didn't say 'that's OK, it's just going into the next room' or any sort of facile things, he said 'Father, if it be possible, let this cup pass from me, nevertheless not my will, but thine be done'. It isn't the story of a serene person; you know, untroubled by circumstances whatsoever.

PM: How – I wasn't thinking of this, but connected with what you've just said – how do you interpret the words from the cross, 'My God, my God, why hast thou forsaken me?'?

JP: As with his death, if Jesus is the son of God and came to share and redeem human nature, then he has to share in all human experience – 'what is not shared is not redeemed', as St Gregory of Nazianzus says, and that's to me a convincing insight. The experience of God's forsaking us IS a human experience, and part of the strange wonder of the cross is that Jesus, despite being the son of God, shares that.

PM: Yes. Do you think it is as strong as 'sharing despair'?

JP: Well it's very much like that. It's very much like that. 'Dereliction.' I mean it's describing dereliction. It ends, remember, with Jesus saying 'it is finished', and that's not a sort of 'ah, thank God that's over' type of thing, it's *tetelestai* in the Greek as you probably know, and that is more a sense of triumph: it is fulfilled, it is *completed*.

PM: Yes, yes. I think an awful lot of people don't realise that.

JP: No, I don't think they do.

PM: The dying of Jesus was terrible, is terrifying. It seems to me a person might not be afraid of death because of what they believe about the world beyond, but they will be very afraid of dying. The sheer number of ways in which you might have to die is terrifying. But coming back to the strange semantics, would it be true to say that for Christians you can't be dead, you can only die? That someone can die but they're not 'dead'? In fact, that you die but there's no death?

JP: Well, there's the Collect for Easter which speaks about death, and about the grave and gateway of death into another life, that's right, yes. Of course you die, that's an inevitable part of all our lives, but it isn't the *closing* of that life. It's not the *end* of that person, not the *end* of life in that false sense. It is clear that the life of the world to come is different from this world, and as I say death is the grave and gate which leads from one to the other.

PM: It seems as though dying is the discontinuity bit, but there's no 'being dead'.

JP: Yes: we're saying that YOU are not identified with the corpse in the grave.

5

A New Universe

'Foretastes of eschatological fulfilment' – Music – Forgiveness – Gordon Wilson and Jill Saward – Love in Dante's 'Paradise' – Purgatory, judgement and redemption as a process – Self-condemnation to hell – 'Nothing of good is lost in God' – An integrated destiny for the whole creation – Different physical fabric of the new universe – Christ's *resurrected* body – Steven Weinberg – The scientist-theologian's case.

PM: So does resurrection presuppose this 'sleep' of death, before we are awakened?

JP: Not necessarily. I mean the time of this world and the time of the world to come are not just sequential, and how they relate to each other is something that is an unsolved mystery. But it's perfectly possible to believe that everyone arrives at the day of resurrection at the same time, so to speak. A time not of our time, but a time of the world to come.

PM: Yes. That's very interesting... I'm inclined to say that it's impossible to imagine and therefore it's very credible! It's possible to *speculate* about the world to come, isn't it, but very difficult to imagine? That's why I think you were so wise in *Hope* to discuss our *this*-life experiences of joy, love and forgiveness as 'foretastes of eschatological fulfilment', palpable intimations of what the life of the new creation might be like. I was particularly interested that you mention music as producing one of the 'experiences of joy, those deep moments of peaceful happiness'.[1] What does music mean to you?

JP: Well I don't listen to very much now, because it gets complicated with my hearing-aid and everything, but I used to listen to a lot of music. I very much like, myself, contrapuntal music.

PM: Is that because you are a mathematician?

JP: Exactly so. And that appeals to me...music convinces me of a reality – or a dimension of reality – which one must call 'beauty'. I've mentioned more than once in print talking to some of my scientific friends, who have taken a rather down-to-earth, materialist view of things, and asking them: 'What do you make of music?' And they can't say it's just, you know, molecules bouncing against the ear.

PM: Ha!

JP: There is a reality about music and a mystery to music, as I say. Bach is my favourite composer. And for there to be music in the world to come there must be time, because music is the most temporal form of art. In *Hope* I quote those beautiful words from one of John Donne's sermons: 'Bring us, O Lord God, at our last awakening into the house and gate of heav'n...where there shall be no darkness nor dazzling, but one equal light; no noise nor silence, but one equal music.'[2]

PM: It's a wonderful conception, wonderful. I'd like to touch on *love* as a foretaste of the new creation in a moment. You see, I am less sure about our experience of human forgiveness as an intimation of it, because I have a problem – I think a lot of people have a problem – with Christian forgiveness as it seems to be understood these days. To put it bluntly, when a Christian forgives without the wrongdoer repenting isn't that just Christian self-gratification?

JP: Well it's recognition of the fact that we are people *ourselves* who need forgiveness. And if the grudges and hurts of this world have received no healing – and we all have to participate in that because it's so to speak a 'social process', it's not just individual people – then there's a starchiness and a sadness in the world.

PM: Mm. I once had a discussion with a Russian Orthodox lay preacher about this, and he was adamant that Christian forgiveness could only happen when the wrongdoer had repented. Thus in the example of the drunken driver that you give in *Hope*, it would not be enough, for the Russian, that the drunken driver acknowledged it was his *fault* that he had killed the parents' child, he would have to *repent* and say sorry before he could be forgiven.

JP: Well I don't think that's right. Think about the two thieves on the cross... Of course, if there is ultimate healing, there is ultimate reconciliation. That means in which both sides have to participate. But I think that forgiveness *does* involve accepting the unacceptable.

PM: On a sort of practical political level, many Russian Christians – I mean from the 'catacomb Church' rather than the official variety – believe that all of Russia's problems of the present are caused by the fact that there has not been a national act of repentance for the Bolshevik and Stalinist genocide. There has been recognition, but not repentance; so there can't be forgiveness or reconciliation... It's an interesting argument when you compare it with South Africa, for instance.

JP: Yes. But I don't think God forces forgiveness on anybody. The sort of ultimate cost of forgiveness is that the wrongdoer *hasn't* repented. Just think of Gordon Wilson, that father in Northern Ireland whose daughter was killed in the IRA bomb outrage at Enniskillen. He didn't pretend that they didn't kill his daughter, he didn't pretend that they'd given up that form of violence, he said 'I bear no ill will, I bear no grudge', he just accepted that, in God's grace.

PM: Yes. But of course there you are: you have people who say 'well, this is meaningless, because they didn't repent, they didn't say sorry, for killing his daughter'. It seems to some people a kind of pacifism, doesn't it? Forgiveness without repentance seems a kind of appeasement.

JP: It's not saying there are no consequences from a wrong act, either for the people who have borne the brunt of the act, or for the perpetrators themselves. I mean what you do is, if you're a sort of person who neither can forgive nor accept forgiveness you're twisting yourself in a very unfortunate way.

PM: Yes, yes, I would certainly agree with you there. But what worries me about this form of forgiveness is that it seems solipsistic – only about the giver of the forgiveness and, possibly, his/her credit in heaven.

JP: Well no, it's very important with 'gratuitous' forgiveness that it is given freely, but it's *not without cost*. It isn't saying 'it didn't cost me anything and what you did doesn't matter'.

PM: Well I think that's the conclusion some people who aren't Christians jump to, don't you think?

JP: Yes, they object to that, obviously. But the act of forgiveness isn't saying 'this was a jolly nice chap really, he's made a little mistake about killing millions of people'.

PM: No, and I mean if a country...if people invade my country and kill thousands of people as has happened in Ukraine, why should I forgive them before they have got out again, said it was wrong, and are genuinely contrite? It seems meaningless to forgive them, some people think.

JP: You *might* forgive them for that. There are people exactly in that situation. I mean the important thing is that forgiveness isn't a sort of 'trading' operation. It is gratuitous in that sense.

PM: Yet God's own forgiveness is conditional upon repentance, isn't it? I am thinking, for instance, of Christ's parable in Matthew 18, of the king and the wicked servant. When the servant first asks the king for forgiveness of his 'debt', he seems repentant, or at least terrified of the consequences, and the king forgives him it. But when the servant promptly goes out and grabs by the throat someone who owes him a piffling amount by comparison, and casts him into prison, it's clear he hasn't repented this action one bit and the king does *not* forgive him the second time but gives him over to the 'tormenters', to hell presumably. I accept 'universalism', that God forgives everyone, but I can't believe God will do that without true repentance.

JP: Well of course forgiveness doesn't mean the...throwing away of reasonable punishment. It doesn't mean that evil deeds don't have consequences, for instance under the law. People who don't accept the proper evaluation of their deeds and are not regretful of them are condemning themselves. Coming back to the parable, the tragedy of their hell is not that an angry God has lost patience with them and said 'off you go!', but they themselves have chosen to do that.

PM: Yes, yes. That, of course, fits the unrepentant terrorist, the unrepentant regime that annexes someone else's country, the unrepentant rapist... But if human forgiveness doesn't require the evildoer to repent, won't it be perceived as saying 'forget it, it doesn't matter'?

JP: If a motorist kills your child because he is drunk, or mobile-phoning, how could you say 'it doesn't matter'?

PM: Quite.

JP: It does matter. Nevertheless, I am not going to hate you as a human being and require revenge.

PM: And of course it must be *particularly* difficult to forgive the motorist if he shows no remorse.

JP: Yes. There are people who can rise to that height, for instance Gordon Wilson in Ireland, and Jill Saward and her father in the Ealing vicarage attack.

PM: Mm. I don't discount 'gratuitous forgiveness' having a delayed effect on the wrong doer. I think it can. When the two boys were killed by an IRA bomb in Warrington in 1993, Gordon Wilson begged the IRA to stop but they didn't, and he described his efforts as 'quite pointless'. Yet ten years after Enniskillen, Gerry Adams did make a formal apology for the bombing. On the other hand, Jill Saward's then boyfriend, who was also beaten up, could not forgive the rapists. He said 'these were acts of pure evil, I can't forgive them'.

JP: Well they were evil acts. Yes.

PM: And he saw no contrition.

JP: Yes, well that doesn't mean – obviously, as this example shows – that forgiveness is bottomless. It's obviously a highly unsatisfactory situation but, I mean, nobody can be forced to forgive and nobody can be forced to accept forgiveness, and the point about accepting forgiveness is that first of all you have to acknowledge there is something to be forgiven.

PM: I just feel that we may have got ourselves into a situation where Christians think 'universalism' means forgiving everyone everything with no questions asked, as a kind of psychotherapy because it does *oneself* good. I accept that repentance may not be a precondition for human forgiveness, but surely forgiveness should be more than solipsistic – I mean surely it should involve some reaching out to the wrongdoer, some attempt at *dialogue* with them over the evil they have committed, and the need for them to repent? How do you feel about these great public acts of forgiveness these days, when Christians come forward on television immediately after a heinous crime, and say that they forgive a murderer or terrorist? A lot of people's reaction to that is not positive. They feel that there shouldn't be this parading of forgiveness.

JP: It's a question of the motivation for coming forward. Is it to show a deep Christian attitude of forgiveness of a real wrong, or is it exhibitionism?

PM: It is one thing that makes people regard Christians as smug, you know?

JP: Yes, of course, yes. And there are some who are!

PM: Nevertheless, I do feel that to be forgiven by another human being for something terrible that one did, and that one bitterly regrets, is to have a foretaste of bliss, of God's forgiveness, as you say in *Hope*.

JP: And it is an act of love and grace. It is God's love and grace acting through us when we are able to do it.

PM: I know you feel Dante's 'Paradise' is the least successful part of *The Divine Comedy*...

JP: Yes, I do. It shows just how difficult it is to say anything meaningful about the world to come from a purely limited human point of view. You can't take God in at a glance. The most successful part of *The Divine Comedy* I think is 'Purgatory', because it shows an unfolding *process* of relationship and interaction with divine reality.

PM: I can understand that, but there is something fundamental to Dante's 'Paradise' that comes very close to your own conception in *Hope*! It has been said that permeating all Dante's experience of Paradise, and his conversation with St Bernard of Clairvaux, is the idea that we are resurrected not for our own sakes, but because other people love and know our unique personhood – we are resurrected for those who love us.[3] And you too stress the 'deep relationality of creation'; the 'significant distinction between a human person (constituted in relationships) and a mere individual (treated as if existing in self-isolation)'; you say that 'the pattern that is me cannot adequately be expressed without its having a collective dimension'...[4]

JP: Yes, but I think it is the divine love, the unrelenting divine love which must be the basis for any truly persuasive belief in a destiny after death.

PM: Actually, that's why I find 'Paradise' the most successful part of Dante's poem. You know, Beatrice's great *agapē* for him, his endless Platonic love for her, St Bernard's adoration of Mary, the two women's inexpressible smiles – the love, the beauty and the ecstasy are overwhelming, they really make me think this is all possible somewhere, that everything is 'moved' by divine love as Dante glimpses in the final lines.

JP: I think behind it all, behind this whole belief that we shall 'see' our loved ones again, lies an important intuition. The whole *notion* really of life after death depends upon belief that nothing of good is lost in the Lord, and one of the great goods of our lives has been those positive relationships that we've had; and I'm sure they will be restored and indeed purified and revived in the life of the world to come, and that's as far as I can say... But it's very natural, and I think right, to expect that, as I say, that good which we had with our loved ones is not gone but will be renewed and expanded in the life of the world to come.

PM: And when our relations with people were not so positive...might we be drawn to understanding why?

JP: I think so, I think so, yes. Yes. I mean, in the end, nobody can be in the position of saying, 'If George is going to be there in the life of the world to come I don't want anything to do with it!' Resurrection involves a purification and that's why notions of judgement, and so on, are an important part of it.

PM: I was very interested indeed to read your penultimate chapter in *Hope*, in which you appear to take up a very traditional eschatological subject: the Four Last Things, i.e. death, judgement, heaven and hell. Judgement is a tricky subject today, isn't it?

JP: It always has been really. I think in fact that judgement is a *hopeful* word. You see, a basic idea which lies behind all the discussion is the recognition that God chooses not to act simply by clicking his fingers, but by process.

PM: Right...

JP: And judgement is an indispensable part of a process of first of all recognising things have gone wrong, and then seeking their redemption and change. Judgement is seeing things as they actually are. The idea of appearing before God on the Judgement Day – again obviously there are lots of very complicated analogical arguments being made here – is not appearing before some celestial Judge Jeffreys who says 'that's it, you're free, off you go', it's recognising ourselves as we really are, that there are things in our lives which are still *unrepented*, and coming to terms with that and realising therefore the need we have for divine grace to repair those things. So, as I say, judgement is a hopeful word, it isn't a word of condemnation. It belongs to a world of redemption, and really...if we don't *admit* that we have many things wrong with us or many things in need of healing and change, then we shall never get it. It's the sort of 'iron man' who says 'I'm me and you have to put up with that' who is cutting himself off.

PM: Is judgement then, really, *continuous* with purgatory and redemption?

JP: Yes, I think so, yes. As I say, resurrection surely involves a purification, and because God works through process there has to be some measure of purgatory in a sensible and not Reformation-times sense. I mean, purgatory obviously got a *terribly* bad name at the end of the Middle Ages, and rightly so because it was grossly abused by people –

PM: And there seems to be no scriptural basis for it!

JP: But again: purgatory is simply saying that the change which is necessary in us is not a question of magic – that God willy nilly waves the divine fingers and we're changed – we have to participate in that change, and that participation is a painful participation, but it's coming to terms with reality to a degree throughout, and that's why I think it's in accord with its due process. I mean, I've given public lectures about these things, usually before Anglican audiences, of course, and people have been very upset when I say I believe in purgatory.

PM: Yes. Well I think your view of purgatory is closer to the Russian Orthodox view, than to the Catholic view. Purgatory doesn't *officially* exist in Russian Orthodoxy, but the notion of hell may be regarded as more of a process. Purgatory isn't a place, but a 'purificatory state', as Sergii Bulgakov calls it, one of a sequence of states...[5] And as you doubtless know, the Mother of God plays an important part in mercy. The Orthodox believe that we all have a 'goat' in us –

JP: Have a what?

PM: A goat! They believe there isn't a human 'sheep' that doesn't have a 'goat' in it: we're not just 'all sheep and all goats'.

JP: Ah yes, of course, absolutely.

PM: And that has to be purified, assuming – which I think is still argued about in Orthodoxy – that the torments of hell don't last forever.

JP: Exactly. What we have to call 'purgatory' is a process. And that's one reason why I find it the most successful part of *The Divine Comedy*.

PM: What, then, is hell?

JP: Well, I think only those who repent enter into a healed relationship, with the benefits of what's going on. I mean, suppose there are people who refuse the divine forgiveness all the time. I don't think God destroys them. They are caught in their own web, in that sense. It's been said that the gates of hell are locked on the inside. If there are people in 'hell', people who resist God's call to forgiveness and healing to the very end, then that's...they have to blame themselves for that. They are not there because God has thrown them away and said 'it's not worth bothering with you any more'. As I said earlier, I don't think God *forces* forgiveness on anybody. People aren't carried kicking and screaming...

PM: They have to be free!

JP: They have to be free, exactly. They are 'self-condemned' if they don't accept the mercy and love of God. And I think the place they are in is grey, not red like an inferno, it's a place of boredom rather than endless torment.

PM: And what about the rest of creation? I mean the created world on this planet other than humans?

JP: Yes, well, I feel sure that – perhaps in a slightly sentimental way – there will be animals in the world to come.

PM: Do you? I do too!

JP: But I don't think every animal ever will be there, and certainly I hope not every virus is there. I mean the important thing is, I think, that Christianity doesn't simply see the whole of created order as a 'backdrop' for the human drama which could then be rolled up and stored away... And nothing of good is lost in God. If there are worthwhile things in the physical world – and I think there are – then they will be retained in some appropriate way. It's difficult to think that the fulfilment of creation, the life of the world to come, doesn't include animal life in it. I have never thought animal life is *simply* a means of getting to human life. It has value in itself.

PM: Oh, that's very interesting.

JP: This is a celebrated conundrum, and of course nobody knows the answer. But when people say, 'I don't want to go to heaven unless my doggy comes with me', they're expressing a real relationship with that animal and what I would always wish to say is that nothing of *good* is lost, and how it finds its further expression is not by any means foreseeable, so...it's an open question but not a ridiculous question. You know, you don't laugh at the person who says to you 'I can't go to heaven without doggy', or you don't say 'my goodness, that's nonsense', you just take it.

PM: What I think is so interesting is that you don't have a doctrinal answer. If you were a Russian priest, you would say: 'Animals have unbaptised souls. FACT. So, of course, these souls will survive in the next world.'

But you lay the emphasis on the human nexus, don't you?

JP: Well, eschatological hope doesn't mean *everything* that exists in this world has to exist beyond it. Again the wait and see, leave it to God argument, though infuriating to critical inquiry, is nevertheless an inevitable result at some stage in this argument.

PM: Yes, but the essence of your eschatological belief is that the whole universe is redeemed. As you say in chapter 10 of *Hope*, 'God must surely care for all creatures in ways that accord with their natures. Therefore, we must expect that there will be a destiny for the whole universe beyond its death'.[6] I can believe that as individuals we access the new creation through our death and eventual resurrection, but how and when does the *universe* access it?

JP: Well, the universe only acts through the deliberate act of its creator. That's not an arbitrary or a magic act. A magic act would be an act which had no motivation other than being a sort of show-off performance. The universe's accession to the new creation is just part of the story: it's part of what it means when we say we believe the world to be a creation and God its creator. The whole burden of my tale is that there is a hope for the universe, that there is a hope for us, because we have a faithful creator and that creator is *not* a capricious magician.

PM: But how do you view the fact that the universe will continue existing long after we and all organic life in it has died out? What could be God's purpose in doing that?

JP: That's a hard question to answer. But I don't think God keeps the world in being *without* a purpose. And I don't think that God will keep creation in being all the time. So if the created world in its evolution and history has fulfilled the purposes of God, then God I think will no longer hold that world in being, it will be succeeded by the new creation, which is of course what we have been talking about.

PM: Yes. But you do accept the timescale, the vast timescale that goes with the scientific perception that the universe will evanesce or 'crunch'?

JP: Yes!

PM: You don't think God will change that, pre-empt it, that God might terminate the universe before its 'natural' end?

JP: I think God *can* change it, but it's a divine choice, and it's not for me to tell God how to do his work, so to speak.

PM: To me it seems bewildering that God would prolong the universe for so many billions of years after all of his precious *living* creation had died out in it. It means our destiny will be separate from the universe's. To many, a single traditional Apocalypse might seem to make more sense.

JP: No, I don't think that our destinies will be separate, because there's the integrated destiny for the whole of creation and we are part of that. This is where the notion of resurrection and a new life comes in. The death either of ourselves or of the universe isn't just wiping the slate clean and starting it again, through the power and concern of the creator it's the fulfilment of a purpose.

PM: I'm very naïve in these areas, but I suppose that we might all die and be held in God's memory, and the universe go on for all these billions of years until it collapses, but if we and the universe enter the new creation at the same time of the new creation the time interval is only a time interval of the present world, not of our new world...

JP: Yes. Yes.

PM: So the universe *could*, as it were, be resurrected, or join the new creation, or however you like to put it, at the same 'new' time as us?

JP: Yes. The new creation will be the redemption of the universe from futility, just as for ourselves it will be our own redemption from the futility of this life, and I think the two go together.

PM: So we are talking of a new spacetime for both us and the universe... But is it possible that there are other universes?

JP: Well that's a separate question. If there are any other universes, they will be there because the creator has willed them to be there and God will have a purpose for them. And if there are inhabitants in those universes there'll be a purpose for them beyond their death as we believe there to be for us beyond our own death.

PM: But as you know, certain astrophysicists rather remarkably speculate on whether we could move to those other universes, not just other planets, but other universes...

JP: Well I don't think anyone's produced a persuasive way of how to do that.

PM: If that were possible, surely, and universes continued to be endlessly created, there would literally be no end to human life in the present creation. It beggars imagination, doesn't it?

JP: Yes, I think it does.

PM: In the last chapter of *Hope*, 'The Significance of the End', you write:

I have argued that the new creation must be endowed with a totally different 'physical fabric' from that of the old creation and, of course, this must be on a universe-wide scale. This consideration implies that, though the new creation is the transform of the old creation, the distinction between the two must be as sharp as that between death and resurrection. The one cannot be parlayed into the other.[7]

This distinction, I must admit, I find difficult to accept. I find the combination of continuity and discontinuity in the human case persuasive and totally acceptable, but the discontinuity involved in the case of the universe seems almost too difficult to imagine, as opposed to the death of the universe full stop, as predicted by science.

JP: Well, of course, 'wait and see' is the answer to many of these questions. For the Christian, the key event is the resurrection of Christ, and that is the seed event from which the whole new creation is going to grow. The reason that the tomb was empty is that the material body of Christ had been transformed into a body of the new creation and all of the new creation flows from that.

PM: Yes, and in chapter 10 of *Hope*, 'The New Creation', you say: 'The significance of the empty tomb is that the Lord's risen and glorified body is the transmuted form of his dead body. Thus matter itself participates in the resurrection transformation, enjoying thereby the foretaste of its own redemption from decay.'[8] Now I suppose some people would say that is a generalisation that you can't draw. You can only say that the matter of Jesus's body was transformed.

JP: Yes, but Jesus was raised from the dead by the power of God his father. And we shall have a destiny beyond death because of the power of our heavenly father, so the two are connected through matter. After Christ's resurrection, there's a sense in which the world of the new creation already exists, alongside the world of the present creation. Eventually the world of the old creation is going to be wholly transformed into the world of the new creation.

PM: If the distinction between the new creation and the old creation is 'as sharp as that between death and resurrection', it is certainly not scientifically predictable or explicable...

JP: No no, absolutely not. I mean, the whole issue of the new creation only arises if you believe that the world makes absolute ultimate sense and that science only describes a part of the process of the world. And that ultimate sense must depend upon God's working to bring it about.

PM: Well without our willing it, we have come full circle – back to Weinberg. What would your short answer be, then, to his perception that the universe is 'pointless'?

JP: I'm sympathetic with the problem he poses. I mean, one of the rewards of doing science is that it gives you an understanding of the history and delicate processes which have turned an initial ball of energy – the big bang – into the whole of space and the sciences. But there's something very unsatisfying in the idea that after all it's going to fall apart again. It's like being shown the plans for a beautiful house and being told that as soon as the building is complete it'll be blown up. So I can understand that. Weinberg deepens the intuition that if the world is going to make sense it must make sense all the time, so to speak. The scientific story doesn't fulfil that, it's only part of the story. I think that his statement about the universe being pointless, as though that's the whole story, means that a scientist, whose instinct is to make the deepest sense possible of things, is *not* satisfied with the scientific facts.

PM: So his is a *metaphysical* perception, then?

JP: Yes, of course. Yes, yes.

PM: You yourself are a scientist-mathematician, but also a believer-theologian, so you are two people, really, in one...

JP: No, well I don't think so, I think they are different aspects of my single person.

PM: Well, of course, I'm not remotely suggesting there is any kind of conflict, or schizophrenia, because we've talked, we know exactly where we are coming from about these things, but at times I think that if I *were* a scientist I would feel twinges of sadness and regret that the universe has to come to an end, and I might be *tempted* to think like Weinberg.

JP: Well no, I don't think so. I mean, one might feel a sort of twinge of sadness that there are no dinosaurs around now...

PM: Ha, that's very good. Whenever I see birds I'm jolly glad the dinosaurs evolved into them!

JP: Yes, exactly. As a scientist-theologian I believe that the beautiful fertilities of the world, which are a reflection of the will of its creator, will not be negated by processes that are themselves an expression of the will of God.

PM: Thank you, John, so much.

JP: Thank *you*, Patrick.

NOTES

Abbreviations

John Polkinghorne and Michael Welker (eds), *The End of the World and the Ends of God: Science and Theology on Eschatology* (Harrisburg, PA: Trinity Press, 2000) = *Ends*

John Polkinghorne, *The God of Hope and the End of the World* (London: SPCK, 2002) = *Hope*

1 The End of the Universe

1 Steven Weinberg, *The First Three Minutes: A Modern View of the Origin of the Universe* (London: André Deutsch, 1977), p. 154.

2 *Ibid.*, p. 155.

3 *Ends*, pp. 27, 20-25.

4 *Ends*, p. 28.

5 *Ends*, p. 220.

6 *Ends*, p. 83.

7 *Ends*, p. 13.

8 *Ends*, pp. 19-20.

2 Is Eschatology Necessary?

1 *Ends*, p. 89.

2 *Ends*, p. 1.

3 *Hope*, pp. 105-6.

4 Michael Polanyi, *Personal Knowledge: Towards a Post-Critical Philosophy* (Chicago: University of Chicago Press, 1958).

5 'It Depends What You Mean by Gaps', *Church Times*, 9 October 2015, p. 26.

6 *Ends*, p. 38.

7 *Hope*, p. 107.

8 Søren Kierkegaard, *'The Present Age' and 'Of the Difference Between a Genius and an Apostle'* (London: Collins, 1969), p. 120.

9 *Hope*, pp. xx-xxi, quoted from A.R. Peacocke, *Zygon* 35 (2000), p. 135.

10 *Hope*, p. xiii.

11 I Corinthians 15. 28.

12 *Hope*, p. 93, quoted from K. Barth, *The Epistle to the Romans* (Oxford: Oxford University Press, 1933), p. 314.

13 *Hope*, p. 140.

14 *Hope*, p. 102.

15 *Hope*, pp. 98-102.

16 *Hope*, p. 99.

17 *Ibid.*

18 *Hope*, p. 10.

3 Hope's Seed

1 Luke 8. 54-55.

2 John 20. 17.

3 *Ends*, p. 12.

4 *Hope*, pp. 54-57.

5 Luke 24. 45.

6 Luke 24. 27.

7 *Ends*, p. 212.

8 John Donne, A Sermon Preached at Whitehall, 21 April 1618.

9 *Ends*, p. 59.

10 *Hope*, pp. xvii, 108.

11 *Hope*, p. 108.

12 E.g. II Corinthians 5. 6-8 and Philippians 1. 23.

13 'L'intervista: Il Cardinale Camillo Ruini', *Corriere della Sera*, 22 September 2016, p. 18.

14 *Hope*, p. xiv.

4 Death Is Real

1 *Ends*, p. 254.

2 *Ibid.*

3 Søren Kierkegaard, 'The Work of Love in Recollecting One Who is Dead', in *Kierkegaard's Writings, XVI: Works of Love*, ed. and trans. by Howard V. Hong and Edna H. Hong (Princeton, NJ: Princeton University Press, 2013), p. 357.

5 A New Universe

1 *Hope*, pp. 97-98.

2 John Donne, A Sermon Preached at Whitehall, 29 February 1628.

3 M.M. Bakhtin, *Estetika slovesnogo tvorchestva (The Aesthetics of Verbal Art)* (Moscow: Iskusstvo, 1979), p. 52.

4 *Hope*, p. 109.

5 Sergii Bulgakov, *Pravoslavie: Ocherki ucheniia pravoslavnoi tserkvi (Orthodoxy: Essays on the Doctrine of the Orthodox Church)* (Paris: YMCA-Press, 1985), pp. 383-84.

6 *Hope*, p. 113.

7 *Hope*, p. 143.

8 *Hope*, p. 113.

Index

APPENDIX:

Two Interviews with John Polkinghorne

JOHN POLKINGHORNE: TWO INTERVIEWS

Questions by Patrick Miles, 13 October 2014 – 19 January 2015

1: LIFE WITH DIFFERENT MOTIVATED BELIEFS

*Was there ever a time when you thought that science and religion were **not** compatible?*

No, there hasn't been. And that's my particular experience. Of course, there remain puzzles about how they relate to each other, but I never felt I was faced with a critical choice either/or, it's always been both/and for me. I want to take science absolutely seriously, and I want to take my Christianity absolutely seriously, and I don't see a disagreement between them that makes it impossible to do that.

*Why do you think people **feel** you can't believe in God and science at the same time?*

I think a lot of people believe that without thinking about it very much. It has become just a commonplace of our society: '*Of course* you have to choose one or the other.' And that isn't helped by the work of fundamentalists on *both* sides. It grieves me very much to see Christian people who refuse the insights of science. But the strident new atheists are equally fundamentalist in their way. I have been very struck by the fact that *The God Delusion* sold millions of copies, because in my view it's a very bad book. Dawkins in that polemical mode is as much of a fundamentalist as people who tell us that the world was created in six days. It's a book full of assertion, rather than of argument and discussion. Yet there are obviously lots of people out there who *really* just want to be told: 'Don't believe in God, just don't worry about it.'

Why do think that is?

I think it's because one of the ways in which scientific truth and religious truth differ is that religious truth is more dangerous. It has implications for how you behave and you live your life. I believe in quarks and gluons as the constituents of matter very fervently but it doesn't really affect my life, whereas my Christian faith does affect my life, in all sorts of ways. It's costly.

Do you think it's possible to 'believe' in science in the same way as one believes, say, in God? They are surely so different that 'belief' isn't the appropriate word?

There are certainly different kinds of belief. What I would say is, that both in science and religion we are dealing with *motivated* beliefs. Some people think that religious belief is just plucked out of the air, or mysteriously conveyed as propositions which God whispered in somebody's ear, but I think that religious belief is motivated just as scientific belief is motivated, but of course the motivations are different because the kinds of belief are different. For me the Bible is not a divinely guaranteed textbook where you just look up all the answers and then parrot them forth, it's much more like a laboratory notebook which records the experience and encounters with a divine reality of generations of people over a long time. Reading the Bible enables us to enter into their experiences.

And presumably when people say they 'believe' in science they mean they believe in the scientific ***method****, but when you say 'I believe in Christ' you are believing in a* ***person****, which is so different.*

Yes. Science is a wonderful activity and marvellously successful of course, but the basis of its success is the modesty of its ambition. First of all, it only asks a single question about *how* the world works, it doesn't ask questions of meaning and purpose and value, or *why* things are the way they are. It deals exclusively with *im*personal experience: that particular dimension of experience where experiences can be repeated at will. That gives science its great secret weapon, which of course is experiment. In principle, you don't believe what a physicist tells you, you go and do it for yourself. Obviously, you are unlikely to have a hadron collider in your back garden –

No!

– but in principle that's the point: it's *repeatable* experience. But we all know that personal experience, truly personal experience, is *never* repeatable. We never hear, say, a Beethoven late string quartet the same way, even if we play the same disc of it. Science is very lucky in having the experimental method, but it would be an incredible impoverishment in our account of reality to say only things that can be repeated *ad nauseam* are things that we should take seriously.

Beneath your approach there seems to be a very deeply held view of the ***unity*** *of knowledge...*

That's absolutely right.

Do you think that the problem is that some people are just not 'hard-wired', I mean in their brain, to speculate about or understand a spiritual dimension? ***You*** *can accept two world pictures, because you see them as part of a single impulse.*

Well we know that a great deal, in fact the majority, of the structure of the brain, is epigenetic and is therefore *formed* during our actual experience, but no, I don't think people are 'hard-wired' in that way. We encounter reality at a variety of levels. Sometimes when I am chatting about this sort of thing with my scientific friends who aren't believers, I say to them: 'what do you make of music?' From a purely scientific point of view, music is vibrations in the air impinging on the eardrum. But that hardly exhausts the mystery of music. And most scientists are very keen on music!

When you decided in 1977 to resign your Chair in Mathematical Physics at Cambridge and enter the ordained ministry of the Church of England, a lot of people assumed you had had a 'conversion' –

Not in the sense of a dramatic reversal. I had to disappoint a number of interviewers who wanted some sort of Damascus Road experience, because in fact Christianity had always been central to my life.

But there have been almost Damascene experiences that affected your faith, haven't there? I'm thinking, for instance, of what you say in your autobiography about Christians praying for you when you were dangerously ill.

Yes, when I was a curate in Bristol I was suddenly very seriously ill, in fact I thought I was going to die...and God seemed very far away then in that sort of *barren* experience. But I felt very conscious of people praying for me: my family, my church, some nuns who were great friends of mine, and so on... I twice had an experience – I wouldn't call it a vision, but a sort of waking dream – in which I saw one of the sisters in the convent kneeling before the altar and praying for me...and I was strengthened by that, and grateful for it. It gave me a bit, a tiny bit anyway, of deeper understanding of the communion of saints.

Reading your autobiography, I also noticed that you said of that time, in hospital, that you 'could not manage to pray'. Why do you think that was?

It's a very well documented fact of the spiritual life that many people go through desert periods in their faith. Mother Teresa, for example, had years of saying, 'Where is God? Why doesn't he speak to me and do something?' It's not uncommon. I think I can see partly why – it's part of spiritual formation to *hold* onto God in the darkness. 'My God, my God, why have you forsaken me?'

I notice that in your books you several times refer to obedience to the divine will. I take it that 'kenosis', which you are particularly interested in, is a form of that?

Well yes, you see I think the concept of kenosis (self-limitation) is very important in theology. If one may venture to say so I think there is a divine kenosis in relation to creation, in that God is not the puppet-master pulling every string, but allows people to be themselves and to make themselves, and indeed the whole of creation in appropriate ways to be itself and make itself.

But do you think that we can apply kenosis to our personal lives? In Orthodoxy, for instance, it's strongly believed that we must ***imitate*** *Christ's self-limitation, but in my experience, in Russia, it can produce a kind of 'dominated and dominator' effect.*

There are dangers of that, but I don't think it inevitably does. I mean a woman who has not married and devotes her life to her ageing father, for example – that's a kenosis, and it's certainly not cost-less. Also, I don't believe we are autonomous people, the peak of whose perfection is to decide everything for themselves, without any concern for what God might be saying to them, or other people. We live in community. We are heteronomous.

How does kenosis relate to two of your other central theological concerns, theodicy and eschatology?

The God of love must give some degree of due freedom to creatures. Freedom that's appropriate to their natures. That means God is not the cause of everything, and that is a kenosis on the part of God. It is omnipotence allowing others to be themselves. And if we understand evolutionary history in this way, it's a great good but it has to be purchased by the possibility of ragged edges and blind alleys. To take a *very* simple example, the driving force of the amazing three and a half billion-year history of life on earth from bacteria to you and me has been genetic mutation.

Yes.

But you can't have genetic mutation producing new forms of life to be selected and sifted through natural selection without having the possibility also of malignancy. So that the fact that there is cancer in the world is not a sign that God is gratuitously incompetent, or uncaring, but that it is the necessary cost of a world in which we people are allowed to be ourselves.

But does cosmic decay and eventual collapse, which science tells us is inevitable, imply a malignancy programmed into creation? Most people find it very difficult to understand a creator who destroys his creation.

If God has brought into being this world which has the openness of structure that enables it to evolve in a free sort of way, then it's going to have a degree of entropy (disorder) in it. There are so many more different ways of being disorderly than orderly, and in the end entropy is always going to win. That's the second law of thermodynamics! But of course, I believe that while God has given freedom to creatures to be themselves and make themselves, that's simply the first *step* in what is basically a two-step creation process.

How do you mean?

First of all God creates creatures that exist at some *distance* from the veiled presence and really are able to be themselves and make themselves. But of course, the eventual purpose is to draw all creatures freely into encounter and exploration with the divine reality, increasingly unveiled. And that's the concept of the new creation, which is pretty fundamental in the New Testament and a concept beyond science's grasp. If you just take the scientifically discerned history of the world, the predictions that science of itself can make, then the world does seem to end in futility rather than fulfilment.

Thank you very much, John. In our second interview I want to focus on your last two books, ***Quantum Physics and Theology*** *(2007) and* ***Science and Religion in Quest of Truth*** *(2011). But may I ask you a final biographical question: do you ever have any regrets at giving up your career in academe?*

No, I don't. I had for a long time thought I wouldn't stay in physics all my life, because you don't get better at mathematical subjects as you get older. And I had seen friends of mine who had been important figures in the subject and the subject had then moved away from them. I'd had a reasonable run for my money. Looking back on it, in some ways it seems a strange thing to have sought ordination, but I'm sure it was the right thing to do and I'm grateful for the sort of life it brought me. I have not given up thinking, hard. My intellectual interests now focus on the border between science and religion.

2: THE 'CLOUDY AND FITFUL QUANTUM WORLD'

One of your best-known statements, from ***Exploring Reality*** *(2005), is: 'It is clear that science has not demonstrated the causal closure of the natural world.' This seems perfectly reasonable, but is it a plea for the 'God of the gaps'?*

I think that's a good question. You have to ask yourself, 'What's wrong with gaps?' There are various sorts of gaps. Some gaps are simply gaps of current ignorance: we don't understand this, we don't know how to do that. A God of those sort of gaps is no God at all. As knowledge advances, he fades away. But there are other gaps which are intrinsic, and some of them are intrinsic in the actual physical structure of the world as science has discovered it, and some of them are intrinsic for reasons connected with metaphysics, rather than science. Take the first ones: modern physics has discovered that there are intrinsic unpredictabilities present in physical processes – that is to say, unpredictabilities not due to the fact that we can't calculate accurately or measure precisely, they are just there!

I notice that several times in your most recent books you refer to quantum reality as 'cloudy', 'fitful', even 'veiled'.

Yes, we have lost the simple clarity of Newtonian physics. Quantum theory can calculate, for example, the *probability* of a radioactive nucleus decaying, but it cannot establish whether this particular one is going to decay in the next hour or so. And then there are gaps of *principle* involved in questions which go beyond science's self-limited power to answer. There are big questions. Perhaps the biggest of these metaphysical questions is Leibniz's great question, 'Why is there something rather than nothing?' Why does the world exist at all, and why do the laws of nature exist with the remarkable properties they have? We know that they have to take a very precise form, if the universe was to be capable of evolving carbon-based life; in fact just producing carbon requires the laws of nuclear physics to take a very specific *quantitative* form in relation to that.

Did God have any **choice**, *then?*

Well, Einstein said that when he went to heaven that was the first thing he was going to ask God! I think the answer is yes, God did. I mean, it's interesting at the end of Stephen Hawking's *A Brief History of Time*, when he's explaining all about the beautiful equations of nature and so on, he then asks the question he should have asked himself earlier: 'What is it that breathes fire into the equations and makes a universe for them to describe?' And I think God *has* chosen the world that we are able to describe in that sort of way.

I've read your **Quantum Theory: A Very Short Introduction** *(2002) several times, and can see why Niels Bohr said that anyone who thought they fully understood quantum theory showed they hadn't begun to understand it. But you yourself explain that much of it is 'unpicturable' and many of its postulated particles haven't been 'observed directly in the laboratory'. So how* **empirical** *is quantum physics?*

Very. The phenomena that we are trying to explain are carefully measured, and wonderfully accurately calculated. We know certain properties of electrons to an accuracy which represents the width of a human hair in relation to the distance between Los Angeles and New York, and that's pretty exact. We have the results, the 'phenomenology' as we physicists tend to call it, we know these are interesting things that go on in the world, they have these suggestive patterns about them. But how do they fit together? How are they consistent with each other? How can we actually use them to gain further understanding...to go beyond where we started? That's when we try to find a theory.

Clearly quantum theory is intensely mathematical. But if, according to Gödel's Theorem, we can't prove the consistency of axiomatised systems like mathematics, isn't quantum physics in danger of being self-verifying but not 'falsifiable', as Karl Popper required a truly scientific hypothesis to be?

I'm pretty critical of Popper's logic of scientific discovery. Falsifiability is a much trickier concept than he really conceded, at least in his original writings. You know, a famous example is: all swans are white, until you go to Australia and then see a black swan. But is it *really* a black swan? Or is it a long-necked duck? I think, ultimately, all physical theories – and in fact I think ultimately all human understandings of the nature of reality – have an element of *commitment* to a point of view which is not *logically* coercive.

But what worries me about quantum physics, string theory, or Hawking's stream of cosmological ideas, is that in the absence of empirical observations or falsifiability they seem more like ***metaphysics****...*

They are not simply unmotivated airy speculations. At the end of the day an appropriate degree of empirical *accuracy* is always going to be required. Dirac once said that it was more important to have beauty in your equations than to have them fit physical experiment. By that he didn't mean the fit didn't matter, but simply that if they didn't seem to match, the experiment might be wrong, or you might have made a mistake in the calculations. Particularly people working in *fundamental* physics are deeply impressed with the order of the world. Not only is it orderly but it is also *beautifully* ordered. The fundamental equations of physics are always found to be expressed in what mathematicians would recognise, and agree about, as being beautiful equations.

That is coming very close to the metaphysical statement of one of Dostoevsky's characters, that 'beauty will save the world'!

Maybe... There's *something* in the role of beauty. The sense of a beautiful equation is significant in physics, but we don't always have the right resources to find the beauty that might be lying behind it all.

I must say, as a layman I find it extraordinary that these very scientific chaps like Einstein or Schrödinger, studying a physical reality, have such fierce metaphysical and aesthetic emotions.

But everyone has a metaphysics. It simply means their world view – and we all have to have a world view. Somebody who tells you, for example, that there's nothing to do with reality other than what physics can tell you about it, hasn't learned that from his or her science. It's a metaphysical assumption. Important interpretative issues in quantum physics demand for their settlement not only physical insight, but metaphysical decision. It has turned out that there are both deterministic and indeterministic interpretations possible of quantum physics.

Turning now to your last two books, ***Quantum Physics and Theology: An Unexpected Kinship*** *(2007) and* ***Science and Religion in Quest of Truth*** *(2011), I was very taken by the sets of parallel processes and concepts that you trace in them between science and theology – the dyads, as it were, of theoretical creativity/christology from below and above; quark theory/humanity and divinity; phase transitions/miracles; quantum entanglement/Trinity, etc. These homologies, as you describe them, clearly do exist, but are you afraid of being thought to argue by* ***analogy****, which philosophers don't like?*

Well, theologians are less reluctant about analogy. Aquinas' *analogia entis* (analogy of being) was a very important part of his theological thinking. The point is, when we have to talk about entities which have properties that are not part of our commonsense experience of the world, we have to make use of analogy to get some sort of grip on things. And of course, when you're thinking about analogies the interesting things are not only the things in common, but also the differences...

But isn't there a danger that your dyadic-homologous approach might suggest science and religion are essentially 'the same' – that Dawkins thinks science proves God doesn't exist, but Polkinghorne thinks science proves God ***does*** *exist?*

Well, that *would* be a mistake! It obviously isn't true. Analogy is not just an equation of identity. Science and religion are both similar and different in their approaches to truth. Putting it in the very simplest terms, science is concerned with an impersonal dimension of reality and has therefore to have recourse to repetition and experiment. And that doesn't exist in any form of personal knowledge, and least of all religious knowledge. So that's a very important dysanalogy from the start. But it doesn't mean there isn't *motivated* belief in these subjects.

I found that in both books you produced a convergence between science and theology that is very persuasive.

Well...convergence is perhaps too strong a word. I say it's consonance.

It seemed to me that, quite apart from their separate arguments, towards the ends of these two books you wanted to make summative statements about certain issues. One of these was physicists' Grand Unified Theories, or what is popularly known as 'The Theory of Everything'...

The Theory of Everything claim is just hubris.

You end the last two chapters of ***Quantum Physics and Theology*** *by stressing that for you trinitarian theology is the true 'Theory of Everything'.*

Well I think theology is the theory of everything because God is the ground of everything. It seems perfectly clear to me that science doesn't answer every question and therefore we have to seek other insights as well. It's not an argument that can be condensed into a sentence or two, but I believe that the most comprehensive way of understanding things is in terms of a theological view. For example, the beautiful equations and deep intelligibility of the physical world are understood as being a reflection of the mind of God. Theology really does have a 'scope' which enables it to be an integrating discipline. That's why I say I think the true theory of everything is theology. But of course that's not a knock-down argument.

I also thought it was courageous of you to end your last book, ***Science and Religion in Quest of Truth****, with a section 'Other Faiths', which you clearly regard as a very important subject.*

Yes, I think after the problem of suffering it's the biggest problem on the agenda and it will take a long time. Religions really *matter* to people and that's partly the source of their destructive influences as well as their fertility. It's a puzzling scene, because world religions are obviously all talking about the same dimension of human experience – the encounter with the sacred – but they do have very different things to say about it. Not just about strictly dogmatic matters, but even about human beings. To the Abrahamic faiths human beings are of unique and individual continuing significance. To our Hindu friends personality is recycled through reincarnation. And to our Buddhist friends, if I understand the doctrine of Anatta right, personal individuality is in fact an illusion which we eventually see through. Now those aren't three sets of people saying the same thing in culturally different ways, they are disagreeing. So there are serious and important problems there which need to be pursued and they're only beginning to be pursued, it seems to me. Nowadays, we can no longer dismiss our brothers and sisters in other faiths as being deluded people in far away countries who don't know very much. They're living down the street and we can see the integrity of their lives. So it's a pressing problem. And a lot of faiths are just beginning to talk to each other. Actually I think, in a small way, science can contribute to that. I've taken part in one or two projects in which people from different faiths and religions met together and discussed what they made of modern scientific discoveries, and that's a useful meeting point, I think.

Well, relating to that, perhaps my last question should be: Do you think there is anything positive that can be said for the great public God controversy of the past decade or so? Do you see any good coming out of it?

I think there's a little good coming out of it, but there's a lot to be regretted in the way in which the debate has been conducted. These are very important and difficult issues – the existence of God and so on – and actually in a back-handed sort of way people like Dawkins have done us a bit of a help by putting that question firmly back on the agenda. But they have not done any good to themselves or anybody else, in my opinion, by the way in which they've done so. Instead of entering into argument, they have just indulged in bluster and assertion.

Thank you, John.

Sam&Sam is an Anglo-Russian publisher founded in 1974.
It has published over thirty literary, theological, philosophical and historical titles in both Russian and English (**samandsam.co.uk**), sometimes in collaboration with other Russian publishers.
The following works are currently in print.
Some are available on Amazon, but all may be purchased at reduced price plus postage and packing by emailing: **bychkovserser@gmail.com**.

Religious and historical

- *Sobranie sochinenii G.P. Fedotova (Collected Works of Georgii Fedotov)*, Moscow, 1996- 2014, 12 vols., 400 Rb. per vol., individual vols available.
- *Sviatye zemli russkoi (The Saints of Russia)*, Moscow, 'Belyi bereg', 2002, 2nd edition, 3000 Rb.
- *Pravoslavnaia rossiiskaia Tserkov' i imperatorskaia vlast' (The Russian Orthodox Church and Tsarist Power)*, Moscow, 2015, 300 Rb.
- *Bol'sheviki protiv Russkoi Tserkvi 1917-1941 (The Bolshevik Persecution of the Russian Church 1917-1941)*, Moscow, 2006, 400 Rb.
- Father Sergii *Zheludkov, Liturgicheskie zametki (Notes on the Liturgy)*, Moscow, 2004, 200 Rb.
- *Stradnyi put' arkhimandrita Tavriona (Archimandrite Tavrion's Calvary)*, Moscow, 2007, 2nd edition, 400 Rb.
- *Osvobozdenie ot illiuzii: Zhizn' i podvig arkhiepiskopa-ispovednika Ermogena [Golubev] (Freeing Oneself from Illusions: The Life and Achievement of Archbishop-Confessor Hermogenes [Golubev])*, Moscow, 2010, 400 Rb.

Literary

- Sergei Bychkov, *Tikhie ogni: Izbrannye poeticheskie perevody, vospominaniia, interv'iu (Still Lights: A Collection of Poems, Verse Translations, Memoirs and Interviews)*, Moscow, 2011, 2nd edition, 400 Rb.
- Iurii Dombrovskii, with illustrations by Boris Sveshnikov, *Izbrannoe (Selected Poems)*, Moscow, 2017, 1000 Rb.
- Sigizmund Krzhizhanovskii, *Mysli raznykh let (Thoughts over the Years)*, Moscow, 2017, 500 Rb.
- Georgii Shengeli, *77 sonetov (77 Sonnets)*, Moscow, 2011, 400 Rb.
- Georgii Shengeli, *Izbrannoe (Selected Works)*, Moscow, 2013, 1000 Rb.
- Mark Tarlovskii, *Izbrannoe (Selected Works)*, Moscow, 2011, 400 Rb.
- Patrick Miles, *George Calderon: Edwardian Genius*, Cambridge, 2018, £30

Printed in Great Britain
by Amazon

64148907R00061